Editor
Kim Fields

Managing Editor
Mara Ellen Guckian

Illustrator
Mark Mason

Cover Artist
Brenda DiAntonis

Editor in Chief
Ina Massler Levin, M.A.

Creative Director
Karen J. Goldfluss, M.S. Ed.

Art Coordinator
Renée Mc Elwee

Imaging
Craig Gunnell
Rosa C. See

Publisher
Mary D. Smith, M.S. Ed.

Fourth Grade
SUCCESS

Reinforce and review standards-based skills

Across-the-Curriculum Activities

LANGUAGE ARTS

MATH

SOCIAL STUDIES

SCIENCE

INCLUDES
BONUS Language Arts and Math activities to get a jump start on Fifth Grade!

Author

Susan Mackey Collins, M.Ed.

Teacher Created Resources
6421 Industry Way
Westminster, CA 92683
www.teachercreated.com

ISBN 978-1-4206-2574-5

© 2011 Teacher Created Resources
Made in U.S.A.

Table of Contents

Introduction

Each time a student enters a new grade, he or she is excited to begin a new curriculum and master a plethora of new and challenging skills that come with that grade. All students are intrigued when they learn something new. Remember how fun it was when you learned to write cursive letters for the first time? Or what about the first time you conducted an experiment in the science lab? How exciting it was to see if your experiment would go the way you planned!

Fourth Grade Success is part of the *Success* series that reminds each one of us how wonderful and exciting it is to begin a new grade. Although each grade contains required fundamentals all students need to master, we must not forget that learning itself, no matter the skill, is exciting. *Fourth Grade Success* helps instill the fundamentals each student will need to be successful academically, but it also captures a student's imagination and love of learning as he or she completes each skill and is ready to move on to the next one.

All lessons in the *Success* series meet the national standards desired by today's most innovative teachers. Activities in this book are perfect for the classroom teacher but can also be utilized by parents hoping to find a way to offer extra practice of skills outside of the classroom. Teachers and parents can select pages that will provide additional practice with a concept, or they can choose pages to teach new concepts. *Fourth Grade Success* includes skills in the following areas:

- **Language Arts**   • **Math**   • **Social Studies**   • **Science**

An answer key is provided for these pages beginning on page 168.

This book has a special bonus section at the end to provide a jump start for fifth grade skills. These bonus sections are provided in each book in the series. As teachers and parents work through the skills in each book, they can easily move on to the next grade level whenever they feel a student is ready. For the regular classroom teacher who has just finished with state testing, this extra section will help ensure all students are moving forward. The bonus section for fifth grade has its own answer key on page 192.

Have a successful year!

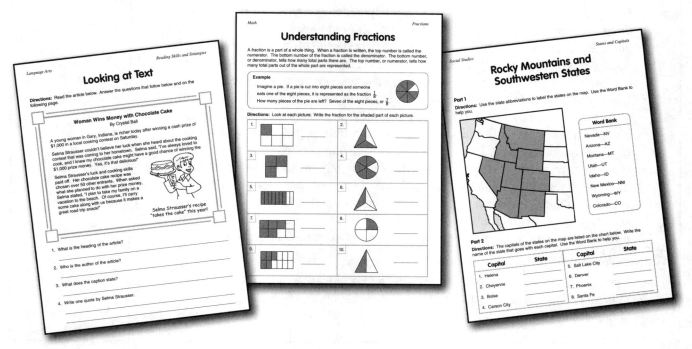

Meeting Standards

Each lesson in *Fourth Grade Success* meets one or more of the following standards, which are used with permission from McREL (Copyright 2010 McREL, Mid-continent Research for Education and Learning. Telephone 303-337-0990. Website: *www.mcrel.org*)

Language Arts	Page Numbers
Uses the general skills and strategies of the writing process	
• Uses strategies to write for a variety of purposes (e.g., to inform, entertain, explain, describe, record ideas)	8
• Uses prewriting strategies to plan written work	9
• Uses strategies to draft and revise written work	10
• Uses strategies to edit and publish written work	11–12
• Uses a variety of sentence structures in writing (e.g., expands basic sentence patterns, uses exclamatory and imperative sentences)	13
Uses grammatical and mechanical conventions in written compositions	
• Writes in cursive	14
• Uses pronouns in written compositions (e.g., substitutes pronouns for nouns, uses pronoun agreement)	15–16
• Uses nouns in written compositions (e.g., uses plural and singular naming words, forms regular and irregular plurals of nouns, uses common and proper nouns, uses nouns as subjects)	17–21
• Uses verbs in written compositions (e.g., uses a wide variety of action verbs, past and present verb tenses, simple tenses, forms of regular verbs, verbs that agree with the subject)	22–23
• Uses adjectives in written compositions (e.g., indefinite, numerical, predicate adjectives)	24–25
• Uses adverbs in written compositions (e.g., to make comparisons)	26–27
• Uses coordinating conjunctions in written compositions (e.g., links ideas with connecting words)	28
• Uses negatives in written compositions (e.g., avoids double negatives)	29
• Uses conventions of spelling in written compositions (e.g., spells high frequency, commonly misspelled words from appropriate, grade-level lists; uses a dictionary and other resources to spell words; uses initial consonant substitutions to spell related words; uses vowel combinations for correct spelling; uses contractions, compounds, roots, suffixes, prefixes, and syllable constructions to spell words)	30–32
• Uses conventions of capitalization in written compositions (e.g., titles of people; proper nouns—names of towns, cities, counties, and states; days of the week; months of the year; names of streets; name of countries; holidays; first word of direct quotations; heading, salutation, and closing of a letter)	33–36
• Uses conventions of punctuation in written compositions (e.g., uses periods after imperative sentences and in initials, abbreviations, and titles before names; uses commas in dates and addresses and after greetings and closings in a letter; uses apostrophes in contractions and possessive nouns; uses quotation marks around titles and with direct quotations; uses a colon between hour and minutes)	37–50
Gathers and uses information for research purposes	
• Uses a variety of strategies to plan research (e.g., identifies possible topic by brainstorming, listing questions, using idea webs; organizes prior knowledge about a topic; develops a course of action; determines how to locate necessary information)	51–52, 56

Meeting Standards *(cont.)*

Language Arts *(cont.)*	Page Numbers
Gathers and uses information for research purposes *(cont.)*	
• Uses strategies to gather and record information for research topics	52
• Uses key words, guide words, alphabetical and numerical order, indexes, cross-references, and letters on volumes to find information for research topic	54
Understands and interprets written and spoken language on diverse topics	
• Uses a variety of context clues to decode unfamiliar words	63
Uses viewing skills and strategies to understand and interpret visual media	
• Understands the different ways in which people are stereotyped in visual media (e.g., clever people wearing glasses, mothers working at home, scientists wearing white coats; superheroes; people from different sociocultural or minority groups) and understands that people could have been represented differently	73–74
Uses reading skills and strategies to understand and interpret a variety of informational texts	
• Knows the defining characteristics of a variety of informational texts	53
• Summarizes and paraphrases information in texts (e.g., includes the main idea and significant supporting details of a reading selection)	55
Uses reading skills and strategies to understand and interpret a variety of literary texts	
• Uses reading skills and strategies to understand a variety of literary passages and texts	57–59
• Understands the author's purpose (e.g., to persuade, to inform) or point of view	64–66
• Understands the basic concepts of plot (e.g., main problem, conflict, resolution, cause and effect)	67–69
• Understands the ways in which language is used in literary texts (e.g., personification, alliteration, onomatopoeia, simile, metaphor, imagery, hyperbole, rhythm)	70–72
Uses the general skills and strategies of the reading process	
• Uses phonetic and structural analysis techniques, syntactic structure, and semantic context to decode unknown words (e.g., vowel patterns, complex word families, syllabication, root words, affixes)	60
• Understands level-appropriate reading vocabulary (e.g., synonyms, antonyms, homophones, multi-meaning words)	61–62

Math	Page Numbers
Uses basic and advanced procedures while performing the processes of computation	
• Adds, subtracts, multiplies, and divides whole numbers and decimals	75–103
• Adds and subtracts simple fractions	106–107, 109
• Solves real-world problems involving number operations (e.g., computations with dollars and cents)	77, 79, 83–84. 100, 103, 109
Understands and applies basic and advanced properties of the concepts of numbers	
• Understands the relative magnitude and relationships among whole numbers, fractions, decimals, and mixed numbers	104–105, 108
Understands and applies basic and advanced properties of the concepts of measurement	
• Understands the basic measures of perimeter, area, volume, capacity, mass, angle, and circumference	110–113. 115

Meeting Standards *(cont.)*

Math *(cont.)*	Page Numbers
Understands and applies basic and advanced properties of the concepts of geometry	
• Understands basic properties of figures (e.g., two-or three-dimensionality, symmetry, number of faces, type of angle)	114, 116
• Understands that shapes can be congruent or similar	117
• Uses motion geometry (e.g., turns, flips, slides) to understand geometric relationships	118
• Understands characteristics of lines (e.g., parallel, perpendicular, intersecting) and angles (e.g., right, acute)	114–119
Understands and applies basic and advanced concepts of probability	
• Recognizes events that are sure to happen, events that are sure not to happen, and events that may or may not happen	120
• Uses basic sample spaces (i.e., the set of all possible outcomes) to describe and predict events	121
Understands and applies basic and advanced properties of functions and algebra	
• Solves simple open sentences involving operations on whole numbers	122–123
• Understands the basic concept of an equality relationship (i.e., an equation is a number sentence that shows two quantities that are equal)	124
• Knows that a variable is a letter or symbol that stands for one or more numbers	122–124
Understands the general nature and uses of mathematics	
• Understands that mathematical ideas and concepts can be represented concretely, graphically, and symbolically	125–129
Understands and applies basic and advanced concepts of statistics and data analysis	
• Reads and interprets simple bar graphs, pie charts, and line graphs	127–129

Social Studies	Page Numbers
History	
Understands the history of a local community and how communities in North America varied long ago	
• Understands the interactions that occurred between the Native Americans or Hawaiians and the first European, African, and Asian-Pacific explorers and settlers in the state or region	130–133
• Knows geographical settings, economic activities, food, clothing, homes, crafts, and rituals of Native American societies long ago	131–132
Understands how democratic values came to be, and how they have been exemplified by people, events, and symbols	
• Understands the basic ideas set forth in the Declaration of Independence and the U.S. Constitution, and the figures responsible for these documents	134, 136–137
• Understands the basic principles of American democracy: right to life, liberty, and the pursuit of happiness; responsibility for the common good; equality of opportunity and equal protection of the law; freedom of speech and religion; majority rule with protection for minority rights; and limitations on government, with power held by the people and delegated by them to those officials whom they elected to office	135–136

Meeting Standards *(cont.)*

Social Studies *(cont.)*	Page Numbers
Geography	
Knows the location of places, geographical features, and patterns of the environment	
• Knows the location of major cities in North America	138–141, 143–145
• Knows major physical and human features of places as they are represented on maps and globes (e.g., shopping areas, fast food restaurants, fire stations, largest cities, rivers, lakes, wetlands, recreation areas, historic sites, landforms, locations of places discussed in history, language arts, science, and other school subjects)	138–145
• Knows the approximate location of major continents, mountain ranges, and bodies of water on Earth	146–147
Understands the characteristics and uses of maps, globes, and other geographic tools and technologies	
• Knows the basic elements of maps and globes	148

Science	Page Numbers
Understands the principles of heredity and related concepts	
• Knows that many characteristics of plants and animals are inherited from its parents (e.g., eye color in human beings, fruit or flower color in plants), and other characteristics result from an individual's interactions with the environment (e.g., people's table manners, ability to ride a bicycle)	149–152
Understands Earth's composition and structure	
• Knows that fossils can be compared to one another and to living organisms to observe their similarities and their differences	153–154
Understands the composition and structure of the universe and Earth's place in it	
• Knows that Earth is one of several planets that orbit the sun and that the moon orbits Earth	155–158
Understands relationships among organisms and their physical environment	
• Knows that all organisms (including humans) cause changes in their environments, and these changes can be beneficial or detrimental	159
• Knows the organization of simple food chains and webs (e.g., green plants make their own food with sunlight, water, and air; some animals eat the plants; some animals eat the animals that eat the plants)	160–162
Understands the sources and properties of matter	
• Knows that matter has different states (i.e., solid, liquid, gas) and that each state has distinct physical properties; some common materials, such as water, can be changed from one state to another by heating or cooling	163–164
Understands forces and motion	
• Knows that magnets attract and repel each other and attract certain kinds of materials (e.g., iron, steel)	165
• Knows that when a force is applied to an object, the object either speeds up, slows down, or goes in a different direction	165
• Knows Earth's gravity pulls any object toward it without touching it	166
• Knows the relationship between the strength of a force and its effect on an object (e.g., the greater the force, the greater the change in motion; the more massive the object, the smaller the effect of the given force)	166
Understands the nature of scientific inquiry	
• Uses appropriate tools and simple equipment (e.g., thermometers, magnifiers, microscopes, calculators, graduated cylinders) to gather scientific data and extend the sense.	167

Purpose of Writing

Directions: Read each statement and circle the correct answer. Write the correct answer on the line and read the completed sentence.

1. A person would write a joke to _____ .

   a. entertain   **b.** inform   **c.** persuade

2. The main purpose of a dictionary is to _____ .

   a. entertain   **b.** inform   **c.** persuade

3. A letter written to the principal arguing in favor of school uniforms is written to

   _____ .

   a. entertain   **b.** inform   **c.** persuade

4. The main purpose of a glossary is to _____ .

   a. entertain   **b.** inform   **c.** persuade

5. An atlas is a book that is written to _____ .

   a. entertain   **b.** inform   **c.** persuade

6. A humorous play is written to _____ .

   a. entertain   **b.** inform   **c.** persuade

Something Extra: In the space below, write three complete sentences. Write one sentence that is *entertaining*. Write one sentence that is *informative*. Write one sentence that is *persuasive*.

_____

_____

_____

_____

_____

Brainstorming and More

A writer *brainstorms* many ideas before he or she begins writing. Do not worry about grammar or punctuation when brainstorming. Do write down many ideas about the assigned topic as quickly as possible. Later, use these ideas to help with the final writing assignment.

Part 1

Directions: Pretend you are writing a paper about which animal makes the best pet. Use the frame below. Decide which animal you would choose and write the type of pet on the title line. Then brainstorm all the reasons why you would choose this pet.

Part 2

Directions: Read your brainstorming section. Circle the five reasons you think are the best for having the animal you chose as a pet.

Use this information to help you write five sentences explaining why everyone should have this animal for a pet. Use a separate sheet of paper or the back of this page.

Something Extra: On the back of this page, draw a picture of the animal you have chosen.

Drafting and Revising

Directions: The sentences below do not have enough detail. Rewrite and expand each sentence to add vivid details.

> **Example**
>
> The cat ran.
>
> The frightened black cat ran up the tree to get away from the dog.

1. My mother laughed.

   _____

   _____

2. The girl swam.

   _____

   _____

3. His soccer team won.

   _____

   _____

4. A mouse hid.

   _____

   _____

5. A breeze blew.

   _____

   _____

6. The bird flew.

   _____

   _____

7. The monster lurked.

   _____

   _____

8. Her stomach growled.

   _____

   _____

Edit for Spelling

Directions: Find two spelling mistakes in each sentence. Circle each mistake. Then write each sentence correctly. Use a dictionary for help if needed.

1. I ate a sandwitch for lunch and some potatoe chips, too.

_____

_____

2. Their is my sister whose taking us to the theater.

_____

_____

3. My favorite class is sceince because we do experiements.

_____

_____

4. I was born on Wedesday in the month of Febuary.

_____

_____

5. There were ninteen children at the birthday partie.

_____

_____

6. What time do you think our pizza delivary will arive?

_____

_____

Writing and Editing Practice

Directions: The following paragraph has at least one mistake in each sentence. Circle the capitalization, spelling, or punctuation mistakes. Rewrite the paragraph correctly on the lines that follow.

① Have you ever been to the beach. ② I love going to the beech. ③ The ocean is beautiful, and the Sun is always so warm and inviting. ④ Have you ever seen the beach at night! ⑤ Its amazing but a little scary, too. ⑥ My favorit thing to do at the beach is to swim. ⑦ It's fun tring to swim when there are so many waves. ⑧ Sometimes my family and I take our floats into the water, and we ride the waves back to the shoar. ⑨ The beach really are a fun place to visit.

_____

_____

_____

_____

_____

_____

_____

_____

Something Extra: On the back of this page, write a paragraph about the beach. Make at least one capitalization, punctuation, or spelling mistake in each sentence in the paragraph. The paragraph should have a minimum of five sentences. Then, with your teacher's permission, swap papers with a classmate and see if he or she can circle the mistakes you made in each sentence.

Writing Exclamatory and Imperative Sentences

Part 1

Directions: Identify each sentence as either exclamatory or imperative. Write the letter **E** beside each exclamatory sentence. Write the letter **I** beside each imperative sentence.

Reminder: *Exclamatory* sentences show excitement or strong emotion. *Imperative* sentences are commands or strong suggestions.

_____ 1. Go to the office, now.

_____ 2. Stop being so ridiculous.

_____ 3. How bright the moon is tonight!

_____ 4. You just won a million dollars!

_____ 5. Get rid of those worms.

Part 2

Directions: Answer each question with an exclamatory or imperative sentence.

1. What should I do with these muddy shoes?

   _____

2. What do you want for lunch?

   _____

3. How do you feel about roller coaster rides?

   _____

4. What is the best gift you have ever received?

   _____

5. Where do you want me to release this snake?

   _____

Practicing Cursive Writing

See how well you remember how to write each cursive letter.

Part 1

Directions: Write the cursive version of each letter beside the printed version given.

1. **A** _____ 6. **S** _____ 11. **E** _____

2. **L** _____ 7. **j** _____ 12. **g** _____

3. **m** _____ 8. **d** _____ 13. **F** _____

4. **t** _____ 9. **Y** _____ 14. **b** _____

5. **z** _____ 10. **k** _____ 15. **D** _____

Part 2

Directions: Write each printed sentence in cursive writing.

1. Friday is the best day of the week.

_____

_____

2. Can you ride a bicycle?

_____

_____

3. What time is it?

_____

_____

4. I wish I could fly like a bird.

_____

_____

Pronouns Take the Place of Nouns

Pronouns can take the place of nouns. Some examples of pronouns are *he, she, it, they, we, me, I,* and *you.*

> **Example**
>
> <u>John</u> passed the salt to <u>Sally</u>.
>
> <u>He</u> passed the salt to <u>her</u>.

Part 1

Directions: Circle the pronouns in each sentence.

1. She is the best cheerleader I have ever seen.

2. Do you think I should go on the field trip?

3. I think he is a wonderful actor.

4. Please give it to me.

5. She is a good friend to me, and I hope we will always be friends.

Part 2

Directions: Use each of the pronouns in the Word Bank at least once in sentences you create. Circle the pronouns in each sentence.

Word Bank	he she it me you

1. _____

2. _____

3. _____

4. _____

5. _____

Pronouns Can Show Ownership

Some pronouns show ownership. Words like *its*, *mine*, *our*, *hers*, *his*, and *theirs* all show ownership. These pronouns are called possessive pronouns. Unlike most nouns, these pronouns do not need an apostrophe to show possession.

> **Example**
>
> *Tom's* car (apostrophe needed)
>
> *His* car (no apostrophe needed)

Part 1

Directions: Below is a list of pronouns. Use a yellow crayon or marker to highlight only the pronouns that are possessive or show ownership.

I	he	his	yours	us	they	mine	ours
her	she	we	it	their	your	its	you

Part 2

Directions: Change each underlined word to a possessive pronoun. Rewrite the sentence on the line.

1. Sadie wanted to go to the dance at <u>Sadie's</u> school.

   _____

2. I think Gage should bring <u>Gage's</u> lizard to the annual pet day in fourth grade.

   _____

   _____

3. Do you think Brett and Terrell know they left <u>Brett and Terrell's</u> scooter at the park?

   _____

   _____

4. The cat purred loudly when Kaitlyn put food in <u>the cat's</u> dish.

   _____

   _____

Singular and Plural Nouns

Most nouns add the letter *s* to form the plural. However, some nouns have different rules for forming the plural of the word. For example, the word *mouse* becomes *mice*, not *mouses*. Use a dictionary whenever you are unsure of how to form the plural of a word.

Part 1

Directions: Change each singular noun into a plural noun. Write the new word on the line.

Singular	Plural	Singular	Plural
1. gift	_____	2. man	_____
3. child	_____	4. kid	_____
5. goose	_____	6. ox	_____
7. box	_____	8. book	_____
9. deer	_____	10. pencil	_____

Part 2

Directions: Change each plural noun into a singular noun. Write the new word on the line. Then draw a picture that represents the singular form of each word.

1. **socks** _____

2. **leaves** _____

3. **foxes** _____

4. **students** _____

More with Singular and Plural Nouns

A red crayon and blue crayon are needed to complete this page.

Part 1

Directions: Each square is filled with nouns.

Use a blue crayon to circle each singular noun.

Use a red crayon to circle each plural noun.

1.			2.		
	goat	oxen		strawberries	peach
	llama	kittens		apples	grapes
	bear	geese		bananas	pear
	turtle	zebra		apricot	lemon
3.			4.		
	noodles	muffin		shirt	pants
	chips	pie		sock	jacket
	crackers	beans		belts	shoe
	cookies	sandwich		sandals	coat

Part 2

Each set of nouns is divided into categories. Decide on a group name for each category.
Write your answers below.

Group 1: _____   **Group 2:** _____

Group 3: _____   **Group 4:** _____

Something Extra: On the back of this page, create your own category of nouns. Be sure
to circle the plural nouns and singular nouns. See if a classmate can guess your category
of nouns.

Common and Proper Nouns

Two types of nouns are common nouns and proper nouns. *Common nouns* are not usually capitalized. They name general people, places, and things. Words such as *girl, mall,* and *desk* are common nouns. *Proper nouns* are capitalized. They name specific people, places, and things. Words such as *Sandra, Eiffel Tower,* and *January* are proper nouns.

Directions: Look at each common noun. Write a proper noun for each one.

Common Noun	Proper Noun
boy	Henry
monument	Statue of Liberty

1. day _____

2. holiday _____

3. month _____

4. teacher _____

5. planet _____

6. doctor _____

7. school _____

8. monument _____

9. building _____

10. state _____

11. city _____

12. country _____

13. continent _____

14. street _____

15. girl _____

16. book _____

17. movie _____

18. language _____

19. mountain range _____

20. actor _____

Unscramble the Common and Proper Nouns

Directions: Unscramble each word. Decide if the unscrambled word is a common noun or proper noun. Write either common or proper noun on the corresponding line. **Hint:** The beginning letter of each word is underlined for you. Capitalize where necessary.

Scrambled Nouns	Unscrambled Word	Common or Proper
1. naa<u>m</u>ton		
2. atr<u>s</u>un		
3. up<u>p</u>yp		
4. el<u>w</u>aonmtre		
5. met<u>s</u>ebrep		
6. one<u>m</u>y		
7. mer<u>s</u>um		
8. soy<u>t</u>		
9. s<u>t</u>ayued		
10. nagaroo<u>k</u>		

Something Extra: On the back of this page, create your own noun scrambles. With your teacher's permission, exchange pages with a classmate and unscramble the nouns. Decide if the nouns are common or proper. Remember to only capitalize proper nouns.

The Subject Noun

The *subject* of the sentence is who or what the sentence is all about. A noun is often the subject of the sentence. A *noun* is any person, place, or thing. There can be more than one noun in a sentence. In fact, a sentence can have many nouns.

Example

Calvin ate pie at supper.

Calvin is the subject of the sentence. *Pie* and *supper* are also nouns, but they are not subject nouns. Remember, the subject noun is who or what the sentence is about. Calvin is the one eating the pie at supper, so Calvin is the subject.

Directions: Read each sentence. Write the subject noun. Then write the other nouns in the sentence.

1.	Katie saw a large snake at the local zoo.
	Subject noun: _____
	Other nouns: _____ _____
2.	Allison sat in the swing underneath the oak tree.
	Subject noun: _____
	Other nouns: _____ _____
3.	Mom baked pizza for the party.
	Subject noun: _____
	Other nouns: _____ _____
4.	The computer is sitting on the table in the library.
	Subject noun: _____
	Other nouns: _____ _____
5.	My cat chased the mouse up the clock.
	Subject noun: _____
	Other nouns: _____ _____

Verbs with Action

Action verbs are words that show something being done or happening. Words like *swim, hop, jump,* and *sing* can all be action verbs.

Part 1

Directions: Circle the action verbs.

sing	candle	mushroom	walked
cloth	yell	cheese	ran
autumn	talked	played	computer
flew	eat	paper	go

Part 2

Directions: Choose any five action verbs from the list above. Use the verbs to create sentences of your own.

1. _____

_____

2. _____

_____

3. _____

_____

4. _____

_____

5. _____

_____

Verbs: Past and Present

Action verbs have tenses. Verbs can show actions that happen in the present or actions that happened in the past.

> **Example**
>
> Colleen *walks* to class.   ➡   *present action*
>
> Colleen *walked* to class.   ➡   *past action*

Directions: Read each sentence. Circle the verb. On each line, write *present* if the verb is a present tense verb. Write *past* if the verb is a past tense verb.

_____ 1. The deer jumped across the creek.

_____ 2. He asked the teacher many questions.

_____ 3. She types extremely fast.

_____ 4. Elle called her mother for help.

_____ 5. Janice takes a break from her work.

_____ 6. He smiles at everyone in the school.

_____ 7. Sunshine makes the day perfect.

_____ 8. The child stomped through the house.

_____ 9. My sister sings in the rain.

_____ 10. Taylor made a terrible mistake.

_____ 11. The train's whistle blows loudly.

_____ 12. He does a good job at everything.

Adjectives: Making Things Interesting

Adjectives describe nouns and pronouns. Adjectives tell *how many, which one,* and *what kind* about nouns and pronouns.

> **Examples**
>
> There are **three** books in the series.   (how many)
>
> I want to show you the **first** book in the series.   (which one)
>
> All the books in the series are **exciting** books.   (what kind)

Directions: Look at each underlined adjective. Decide if the adjective tells *how many, which one,* or *what kind* about the noun. Write your answer on the line provided.

1. This watch was my grandfather's favorite.

   Adjective: _____

2. I was awarded last place in the science fair, but there were only three contestants.

   Adjective: _____

3. There are many reasons why we should go to the fair.

   Adjective: _____

4. I have several pages of homework I need to complete.

   Adjective: _____

5. The sticky lollipop was stuck to my shoe!

   Adjective: _____

6. Twenty children signed up for the field trip.

   Adjective: _____

7. These cookies are for the bake sale.

   Adjective: _____

8. I think he is a funny comedian.

   Adjective: _____

Something Extra: On the back of this page, choose any three of the underlined adjectives. Write sentences of your own using the adjectives you choose.

Choosing Great Adjectives

Directions: Circle the adjective that best completes each sentence. Write your answer choice on the line.

1. He is the _____ person I know; he has won the math contest the last four years.

   a. funniest   **b.** smartest

2. Our teacher said there would be a first, second, and _____ place in the contest.

   a. third   **b.** winning

3. Ken likes to eat crunchy cereal, but Karen likes to eat _____ cereal.

   a. crispy   **b.** soggy

4. She is the _____ teacher because she always has such fun ideas.

   a. worst   **b.** greatest

5. Please give me _____ book.

   a. that   **b.** these

6. It takes _____ hours to complete a long project.

   a. many   **b.** few

7. I wish I had _____ shoes.

   a. those   **b.** that

8. I am glad you are my _____ friend.

   a. mean   **b.** best

Something Extra: Think about your favorite food. On the back of this page, draw and color a picture of your favorite food. Then list three adjectives to describe it.

Learning Adverbs

Adverbs tell how, when, where, and to what extent about verbs, adjectives, and other adverbs. Many adverbs end in the letters *-ly*. However, not all adverbs end in these two letters, and some words that end in the letters *-ly* are not adverbs.

> **Examples**
>
> He moved **quickly** through the house.   →   how
>
> My birthday was **yesterday**.   →   when
>
> **There** is my coat.   →   where
>
> She is **very** nice to me.   →   to what extent

Part 1

Directions: Each sentence contains two adverbs. Circle the two adverbs in each sentence.

1. Yesterday I left my sweater here at the school.
2. I was very excited to see you there.
3. The princess lived very happily with the prince.
4. Move away quickly from the door.
5. He moves too slowly to win the race.

Part 2

Directions: Complete the chart to show the *comparative* and *superlative* degrees of each adverb listed. The first one has been done for you.

Note: Some of the words below can be used as other parts of speech.

Positive	Comparative	Superlative
1. hard	harder	hardest
2. slow	_____	_____
3. quick	_____	_____
4. soft	_____	_____
5. loud	_____	_____
6. fast	_____	_____

Something Extra: On the back of this page, draw a picture of a turtle being faster than a rabbit. Write a sentence to describe your picture. Use at least one adverb in your sentence. Then circle the adverb.

Adverbs, Adverbs, Adverbs

Adverbs are words that describe verbs, adjectives, or other adverbs.

Directions: Write an adverb to complete each sentence. (Do not use the same adverb more than once.) Rewrite the sentence, with the adverb you have chosen, on the lines provided.

1. Cameron walked _____ to the bank to get there before it closed.

   _____

   _____

2. He is _____ short for his age, and most of his friends are taller than he is.

   _____

   _____

3. The rain fell _____ during the night.

   _____

   _____

4. A breeze blew _____ through the trees.

   _____

   _____

5. My friends are always _____ nice to my parents.

   _____

   _____

6. When I get nervous, I always speak too _____ .

   _____

   _____

7. Do you think we will _____ be friends?

   _____

   _____

8. I have _____ been to the ocean.

   _____

   _____

Conjunctions: Connecting Words

Conjunctions are words that connect other words, phrases, and even sentences. The words *and, but, or, nor, for, yet,* and *so* are conjunctions.

Directions: Circle the conjunction that best completes each sentence.

1. My mother (and, but) my father are going to chaperone the dance.

2. I like pancakes, bacon, (yet, and) sausage for breakfast.

3. Neither rain (or, nor) snow will stop our camping trip.

4. He is my friend, (yet, or) he sometimes makes me upset.

5. I will finish my homework, (but, so) I may have free time.

6. I like to go fishing, hiking, (nor, and) bicycling.

7. You need to either get a new backpack, (or, nor) repair the old one you have.

8. Dad gave my sister and me nearly identical bicycles, (but, nor) my sister's is red and mine is blue.

9. People are basically the same, (but, for) all people share similar emotions.

10. Calvin wanted to go to the beach, (and, but) it would not stop raining.

11. You can invite Jennifer, Karen, Olivia, (and, or) Michele, but you cannot invite all of them.

12. I like to watch scary movies, (but, nor) I am still scared when the movies are over!

13. Either you clean your room (nor, or) you are in trouble.

14. My sister (and, or) my brother are both going with me.

Watch Those Negative Words

When you write, avoid using double negatives. Words such as *never*, *not*, *no*, *hardly*, *scarcely*, and *nothing* are all examples of negative words.

> **Examples**
>
> I *hardly ever* eat candy. (correct)
>
> I *hardly never* eat candy. (not correct)

Part 1

Directions: Look at the list of words inside each lens. Circle only the negative words.

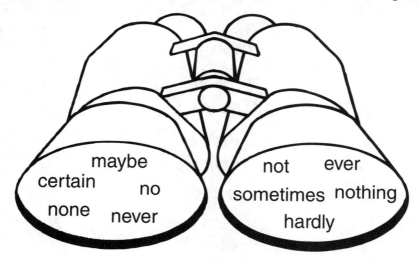

maybe
certain   no
none   never

not   ever
sometimes   nothing
hardly

Part 2

Directions: Use four of the words you have circled. Write sentences that contain only one negative word in each sentence. Circle the negative word in each new sentence.

1. _____

_____

2. _____

_____

3. _____

_____

4. _____

_____

Sweet Compound Words

A *compound word* is a word that is a combination of other words. *Cupcake* is an example of a compound word. The word *cup* and the word *cake* are combined to create the new word *cupcake*.

Materials for pages 30–31

- scissors
- crayons
- sheet of unlined paper or construction paper

Part 1

Directions: Look at the word list below. Combine pairs of words to create eight new compound words. Write the new compound words on the lines below.

basket	sun	butter
super	handy	stairs
down	space	plane
gloss	bug	hair
flower	ball	bow
house	dragon	shine
cup	man	up
grass	lip	lady
air	rain	ship
doll	fly	star
stick	foot	base

Compound Words

1. _____   2. _____

3. _____   4. _____

5. _____   6. _____

7. _____   8. _____

Sweet Compound Words (cont.)

Part 2

Note: Use the compound words created on page 30 to complete the activity below.

Directions: Color the cupcakes on this page. Cut out each cupcake and write a compound word on the line. Glue the completed cupcakes onto a piece of unlined paper or construction paper.

Correct Contractions

Apostrophes are used to form contractions. A *contraction* is a shortened version of two words which are put together to make one new word.

> **Examples**
>
> could have → could've

Part 1

Directions: Form the correct contraction for each set of words.

1. is not _____

2. should have _____

3. you would _____

4. will not _____

5. she will _____

6. he would _____

7. are not _____

8. I would _____

9. he will _____

10. I am _____

Part 2

Directions: Circle the contraction in each sentence. Add the apostrophe needed for each one. Rewrite the word with the apostrophe on the line below the sentence.

1. I do not think Ill ever forget the time you did the comedy routine in the talent show.

   _____

2. You should agree that shes an extremely nice person.

   _____

3. Isnt your brother the quarterback of the football team?

   _____

4. Hes my best friend.

   _____

5. He was so full, he couldnt eat another bite.

   _____

32

Capitalization: Making the Right Choice

Proper nouns should always be capitalized. *Proper nouns,* unlike common nouns, name specific people, places, and things. Examples of proper nouns include the names of people, streets, cities, counties, states, countries, continents, days of the week, months, and holidays.

Common Nouns	Proper Nouns
month	February
ocean	Atlantic Ocean
street	Oak Wood Street

Directions: Each sentence has at least one capitalization mistake. Find each word that should be capitalized. Circle the word(s), and then rewrite the sentence with correct capitalization.

1. My sister's birthday is next april.

   _____

2. I live at 321 elm street in ashland city, Tennessee.

   _____

3. For vacation, we are taking a cruise around some of the islands in the pacific ocean.

   _____

   _____

4. Yesterday, I asked my mother if we could take our vacation in europe, but she said she wanted to go to australia.

   _____

   _____

5. It often snows during the month of january.

   _____

6. My parents' best friends are jerry and betty boyte.

   _____

7. I think kelly and chondra are going to the party.

   _____

8. Canada is a neighbor to the united states of America.

   _____

Capitalizing in Quotes

In a quotation, the first word after the first quotation mark is always capitalized.

> **Example**
>
>   Kip said, "<u>P</u>lease give me your answer."
>
> Notice the letter *p* is capitalized even though it is in the middle of a sentence. *Please* is the first word of the quotation; therefore, it should be capitalized.

Directions: Each quotation has a capitalization error. Find the mistake. Then, draw three lines under the letter that should be capitalized, and write the capital letter above the lowercase letter. See the example below.

> **Example**
>
>   ^Y
>   Carlos said, "<u>y</u>ou should always be careful when you drive."

1. "don't you wish," Kate asked, "that the weekend was one day longer?"

2. Kevin said, "today is my birthday."

3. "please give me that book," the librarian said.

4. Andrea stated, "it is a beautiful day."

5. The teacher said, "please get out your homework."

6. "the puppy ate all his food," Josh told his mother.

7. "why don't you like broccoli?" Katie asked her sister.

8. "i wish I could learn to ride a horse," Selena sighed.

9. "this has been a very special day," whispered Dad.

10. Sam yelled, "watch out for the ball!"

Writing Letters and Capitalization

Directions: Read the friendly letter below. Circle any capitalization mistakes on this page. Then on your own paper, rewrite the letter, correcting any capitalization errors. There are 10 capitalization mistakes in the letter.

123 morgan road

hoppy town, TN 12345

september 12, 2011

Dear anne,

    How are you? i am doing fine. I hope you will come to see us again soon. It was a lot of fun having you spend the holidays with us. Mom says we may be able to travel to kentucky soon and see you at your house. If so, we'll call you, of course, before we come.

yours truly,

terry

Writing a Letter with Correct Capitalization

Directions: Use the outline below to write a friendly letter to anyone in your class (including your teacher). Be sure to use correct capitalization. Include information in your letter that tells about things that have happened recently in your class. If you do not want to use your own address, you can create a new one, but you must still follow the rules of capitalization.

Something Extra: When you are finished with your letter, share it with a classmate. See if he or she can find any mistakes. Correct any mistakes before turning in your work.

End Marks

Directions: Add the correct ending punctuation for each sentence. Write the punctuation mark inside the box at the end of each sentence. Be sure to choose the correct ending punctuation mark.

> **Ending Punctuation Marks**
>
> Question Mark   **?** →   for questions
>
> Period   **.** →   for mild commands or statements
>
> Exclamation Point **!** →   for excitement or emotion

1. Summer is my favorite season ☐

2. Do you like summer, too ☐

3. In the summer there is swimming, camping, and hiking ☐

4. How wonderful the season is ☐

5. One summer when I went hiking, I almost stepped on a poisonous snake ☐

6. Watch where you step ☐

7. Have you ever seen a snake ☐

8. My mother's favorite season is winter because the snakes hibernate in the cold weather ☐

9. Winter is a fun season ☐

10. Watch out for snowball fights ☐

11. Do you like building snow forts ☐

12. Whatever the season, I always have fun ☐

Abbreviations

Directions: Add a period as needed for each abbreviation. Rewrite the abbreviations.

1. Dr Sanders

_____

2. Mrs Smith

_____

3. 761 Ellington Dr

_____

4. 12 in

_____

5. Washington, DC

_____

6. Jan and Feb

_____

7. Gen Washington

_____

8. Mr Thompson

_____

9. Hwy 49

_____

10. Cherry Ln

_____

11. Sept and Oct

_____

12. Oak St

_____

13. Ms Evans

_____

14. Lt Brown

_____

15. Toyville Inc

_____

16. Capt Hitt

_____

17. Cannon Blvd

18. Martin Luther King, Jr

Something Extra: On the back of this page, write a sentence using two abbreviations.

Short Stuff

Directions: Find the abbreviation in each sentence. Circle each abbreviation. Then write the word the abbreviation represents on the line below the sentence.

1. I live at 12 Partridge Ave.

   _____

2. Mr. Bush assigned us a report for science class.

   _____

3. Capt. Sawyers told the troops they would leave for Europe next week.

   _____

4. My father works at Automation Inc. in Springfield, Missouri.

   _____

5. My birthday is in Nov.

   _____

6. Please have the report to me by next Wed.

   _____

7. Our school is located at 123 Old Clarksville Rd.

   _____

8. Braxton Edward Jamison, Jr. will be the guest speaker at the reception.

   _____

Something Extra: List three abbreviations not used in the sentences above: _____, _____, _____. Then see if another classmate knows the correct word for each abbreviation.

Using Commas with Dates and Addresses

Commas are used to separate dates from the rest of the sentence. Commas are also used to separate parts of an address.

> **Examples**
>
> Today is Tuesday, June 5, 2011.
>
> Today is Tuesday, June 5, 2011, which is my birthday.
>
> She lives at 123 Anderson Lane, Happy City, New Hampshire, in the northern section of the United States.

Directions: Read each set of sentences. Circle the sentence in each set where commas are correctly used.

1.	**a.** My parents' anniversary is June 8, 1991.
	b. My parents' anniversary is, June 8, 1991.
2.	**a.** The address for the doctor is 121, Elm Street, Toon Town, Mississippi.
	b. The address for the doctor is 121 Elm Street, Toon Town, Mississippi.
3.	**a.** The invitation states that the party is Friday April, 26.
	b. The invitation states that the party is Friday, April 26.
4.	**a.** The twins were born on Sunday March 3, just one day before their grandmother's birthday.
	b. The twins were born on Sunday, March 3, just one day before their grandmother's birthday.
5.	**a.** Please deliver the package to 321 Ashwood Lane Summer City Michigan.
	b. Please deliver the package to 321 Ashwood Lane, Summer City, Michigan.

Something Extra: On the back of this page, write one sentence with your address and one sentence with your date of birth. Be sure to use commas correctly in each sentence.

Commas in Parts of a Letter

Directions: Add commas as needed. Then correctly label each part of the letter (date, salutation, closing).

1. Dear Thomas   _____

2. Sincerely   _____

3. Love always   _____

4. Dear Mom   _____

5. Cordially yours   _____

6. October 18 2008   _____

7. Yours truly   _____

8. Dear Linda   _____

9. Tuesday November 11 2000   _____

10. Always yours   _____

11. Dear Grandmother   _____

12. January 1 1931   _____

Commas in a Letter

Directions: The letter below has four comma errors. Circle the section where each comma should be. Then rewrite the letter correctly on the lines provided.

321 Shadowbrook Lane
Happy City New York 54321
July 19 2011

Dear Cheyenne

    I wanted to thank you for letting me come to your house last Friday to ride horses. Sugar is the prettiest horse I have ever seen. She was so gentle. I loved feeding her from the palm of my hand. Thank you, too, for inviting me again next month. I will definitely come back and ride with you.

Sincerely

Hannah

_____

_____

_____

_____

_____

_____

_____

_____

_____

_____

_____

Apostrophes to Show Ownership

An *apostrophe* (') can be used to show ownership or possession.

Examples

Darren's basketball

the family's house

the dogs' owners

Directions: Read each phrase. Correct each phrase using an apostrophe. Then write a sentence using each phrase. Be sure to use an apostrophe to show ownership.

Example

the cats collar ➔ the cat's collar

I think the cat's collar is getting too small.

1. the childrens toys _____

_____

2. a girls doll _____

_____

3. the houses alarm _____

_____

4. the geeses feathers _____

_____

5. a persons problems _____

_____

6. the students backpacks _____

_____

Silly Sentences with Apostrophes and Possession

Part 1

Directions: Draw a line to match each animal in the left column to a corresponding word in the right column. There are no right or wrong answers, but whatever sets are matched will be used in Part 2.

monkey	bugs
frogs	fur
puppies	pizzas
camels	toys
rabbit	earrings

Part 2

Directions: Use four of the matched sets from Part 1 to create silly sentences. Use the sets you created to show ownership. Remember to include an apostrophe in each sentence.

> **Example:** elephants   trumpets
> The *elephants' trumpets* make beautiful music that the lions love to hear.

1. _____

   _____

2. _____

   _____

3. _____

   _____

4. _____

   _____

Colons

Colons can be used in many different ways.

> **Examples**
>
> 3:1 ➔ in a **ratio**
>
> 4:30 ➔ between the hour and the minutes **to tell time**
>
> John 1:17 ➔ between the book and the verse of **religious texts**
>
> Dear Sir: ➔ after the **salutation** in a business letter
>
> Bring the following: eggs, milk, and cheese. ➔ to **introduce a list**

Directions: Add a colon as needed in each sentence or phrase. Rewrite the sentence or phrase using the colon.

1. At the wedding, the preacher read from Matthew 3 2. _____

   _____

2. Please bring the following items glue, scissors, and markers. _____

   _____

3. Dear Madam_____

4. Meet me at the store at 7 30.

   _____

5. Dear Mr. and Mrs. O'Dell _____

6. The ratio on the math worksheet was written as 2 1. _____

   _____

7. Does the movie start at 2 30 or 2 45?

   _____

8. Dear Sir_____

9. Mrs. Coffman invited the following students to go on the trip Lisa, Jackson, and Bill.

   _____

10. The rules are as follows no talking and no running.

    _____

Titles That Need Quotation Marks

Short works include poems, short stories, songs, chapters, and television episodes. Short works need quotation marks around their titles.

> **Example:** "Winter Wonders" is my favorite poem.

Directions: Read each sentence. Add quotation marks as needed.

1. My favorite poem is A Little Light by Chonda Roddy.

2. I love the book, but chapter 11, Silverman and Me, is a little boring.

3. Mrs. Addison told us to read A Night of Right, a short story by Josh Tillman, for homework.

4. Love Is Funny is a hilarious poem that everyone should read.

5. At the party, I heard my favorite song, Join the Band.

6. Will you sing Love Isn't Fair with me at the talent show?

7. We had to outline chapter 4, Electric Power, in science class.

8. Have you seen the episode Creepy Crawlers on *The Nature Show*?

9. We like to dance to Hip Hop Happy during recess.

10. Did you watch Sing Song Sally when you were little?

Something Extra: Answer each question in a complete sentence. Use quotation marks correctly.

What is your favorite song? _____

_____

What is your favorite poem? _____

_____

Quotation Marks and Titles

Quotation marks are used around the titles of short works such as chapter titles, poem titles, short story titles, and song titles.

Directions: List five titles for each category. Write the titles in quotation marks. Use the library or Internet (with the teacher's permission) as needed to research titles.

Song Titles	Poem Titles
1. _____	1. _____
2. _____	2. _____
3. _____	3. _____
4. _____	4. _____
5. _____	5. _____
Chapter Titles	**Short Story Titles**
1. _____	1. _____
2. _____	2. _____
3. _____	3. _____
4. _____	4. _____
5. _____	5. _____

Quotes and Quotation Marks

Place quotation marks around a person's exact words.

> **Examples**
>
> Olivia said, "I love peanut butter."
>
> "I think peanut butter is gross," Kevin replied.

Directions: Add quotation marks where they are needed in each sentence.

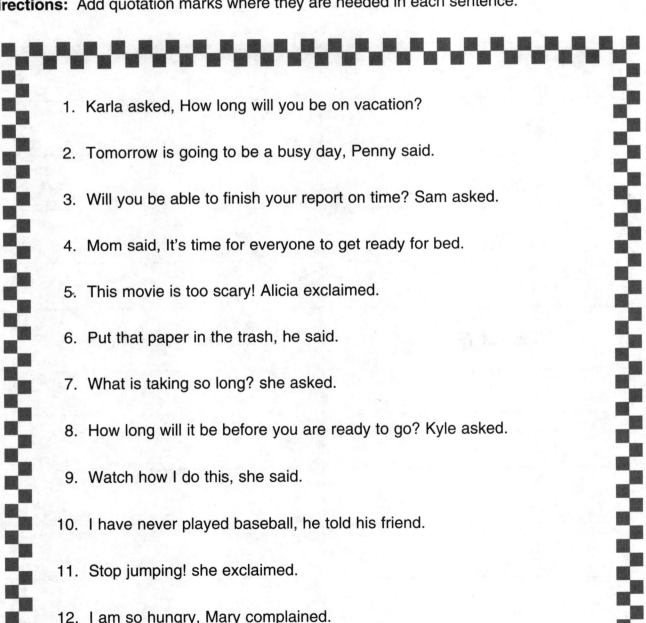

1. Karla asked, How long will you be on vacation?

2. Tomorrow is going to be a busy day, Penny said.

3. Will you be able to finish your report on time? Sam asked.

4. Mom said, It's time for everyone to get ready for bed.

5. This movie is too scary! Alicia exclaimed.

6. Put that paper in the trash, he said.

7. What is taking so long? she asked.

8. How long will it be before you are ready to go? Kyle asked.

9. Watch how I do this, she said.

10. I have never played baseball, he told his friend.

11. Stop jumping! she exclaimed.

12. I am so hungry, Mary complained.

She Said, He Said

Quotation marks are placed around a person's exact words.

> **Example**
>
> She asked, "What is wrong with this page?"

Directions: Circle the sentence in each set with quotation marks that are used correctly.

1.	**a.** He said, "I like going to Florida."
	b. "He said, I like going to Florida."
2.	**a.** "How much money does it cost? she asked."
	b. "How much money does it cost?" she asked.
3.	**a.** Potato soup is my favorite soup, "Robert said."
	b. "Potato soup is my favorite soup," Robert said.
4.	**a.** "Why isn't the weekend longer?" Charlie asked.
	b. Why isn't the weekend longer?" Charlie asked.
5.	**a.** "We aren't ready to go, he said.
	b. "We aren't ready to go," he said.
6.	**a.** "I want to" take swimming lessons, Emily said.
	b. "I want to take swimming lessons," Emily said.
7.	**a.** "Yesterday was my birthday," Shondra said.
	b. "Yesterday" was my birthday, "Shondra said.
8.	**a.** "Everyone did a great job! the teacher exclaimed."
	b. "Everyone did a great job!" the teacher exclaimed.

Something Extra: In the space below, make up answers for questions 2 and 4 above. Use quotation marks around your exact words.

Answer to #2: _____

_____

Answer to #4: _____

_____

Quotation Marks: Mixed Review

Directions: There are quotation mark errors in each sentence. Rewrite each sentence by adding quotation marks as needed.

1. Summer Magic is a short but wonderful poem.

    _____

    _____

2. Mr. Rosetta asked the class, Who is finished with the assignment?

    _____

    _____

3. Why are you so upset? Jeff asked.

    _____

4. I enjoyed the article, How to Train Your Dog, in Friday's newspaper.

    _____

    _____

5. My favorite song is You and Me.

    _____

6. Please be quiet in the library, she said.

    _____

7. Are you going to be late? he asked.

    _____

8. Look out! she yelled.

    _____

Narrowing Down an Idea

Directions: Circle the most specific research topic in each section.

1.
- **a.** The Civil War
- **b.** Soldiers of the South
- **c.** General Robert E. Lee's Surrender
- **d.** Women Who Fought in the Civil War

2.
- **a.** The Scientific Method
- **b.** Science Curriculum for Fourth Graders
- **c.** Project Ideas for Science Fairs
- **d.** Creating Invisible Ink

3.
- **a.** The Presidents of the United States
- **b.** George Washington Becomes President
- **c.** The Executive Branch of the Government
- **d.** Vice Presidents Who Became Presidents

4.
- **a.** The First Female U.S. Senator
- **b.** The Senate and the House of Representatives
- **c.** The Legislative Branch of Government
- **d.** Senators from the State of Tennessee

5.
- **a.** Molly Pitcher's Heroic Efforts
- **b.** The Revolutionary War
- **c.** British Generals of the Revolutionary War
- **d.** Famous Battles of the Revolutionary War

Something Extra: Imagine your teacher has assigned you a science report. The report must be about plants or animals. The report can be no longer than two pages. You are allowed to choose the specific topic. What topic would you chose for your report?
Hint: Remember to be specific.

Topic: _____

KWL Charts

A *KWL chart* is a great way to organize information about a topic when you are first beginning a unit of study.

In the KWL chart, *K* stands for *know,* or what you already know about the topic.

W stands for *want*, or what you want to learn about the topic.

L stands for *learned*, or what you have learned about the topic when the unit has ended.

Directions: Use the KWL chart below to help you complete information about a new unit your teacher is beginning in class. If you need more space, use the back of the page.

K	W	L
1. _____ _____ _____	_____ _____ _____	_____ _____ _____
2. _____ _____ _____	_____ _____ _____	_____ _____ _____
3. _____ _____ _____	_____ _____ _____	_____ _____ _____

Finding Sources

When researching a topic, you should use the most reliable source you can find. A *reliable source* is a source that supplies accurate and detailed information.

Directions: Circle the the most reliable source for each situation below. Write the correct answer on the line and read the completed sentence.

1. Information for a report about the physical features of Italy could best be found in

   _____ .

   a. a thesaurus **c.** a newspaper tabloid
   b. an atlas **d.** a dictionary

2. Information on how to give a dog a bath could best be found in

   _____ .

   a. an article about grooming one's dog **c.** an almanac
   b. an encyclopedia **d.** a thesaurus

3. Information about the early life of Abraham Lincoln could best be found in

   _____ .

   a. an encyclopedia **c.** a glossary
   b. an autobiography **d.** a dictionary

4. Information about making a paper airplane could best be found in

   _____ .

   a. an encyclopedia **c.** an article about designing paper airplanes
   b. an atlas **d.** a manual on how to fly a remote-controlled airplane

5. Information about the planet Saturn could best be found in

   _____ .

   a. an earth science textbook **c.** a blog about the universe
   b. an atlas **d.** a presentation about the Milky Way Galaxy

Alphabetical Order

Information in research books is often organized alphabetically. Use the activity below to make sure your alphabetizing skills are on track!

Directions: Look at the word list in each box. Write those words in alphabetical order.

1.

_____   atlas

_____   encyclopedia

_____   Internet

_____   glossary

_____   index

2.

_____   textbook

_____   dictionary

_____   thesaurus

_____   almanac

_____   magazine

3.

_____   research

_____   topic

_____   paragraph

_____   sentence

_____   conclusion

4.

_____   punctuation

_____   capitalization

_____   quotations

_____   penmanship

_____   grammar

Paraphrasing Quotes

To *paraphrase* is to state a quote in your own words. A *quote* is someone's exact words. A quote must be written in quotation marks to show that the words are the exact words of the speaker.

Directions: Draw a line to match each direct quote to its paraphrased version.

1. "The beauty of the sun eclipses the moon."

2. "Winter's snow blankets the ground."

3. "Everything is possible for those who believe it can be achieved."

4. "Summer is the season of splendor."

5. "Knowledge opens the mind to many wondrous possibilities."

6. "Always strive to do the best you can do."

a. Summer is filled with many beautiful things.

b. Learning about many different things helps a person know there are many choices he or she can make.

c. A person should always do the best he or she can do.

d. A sunny day is prettier than a beautiful night.

e. When snow falls, it covers the earth.

f. Persons can reach their dreams if they believe it can be done.

Something Extra: Find a quote you really like. Write the quote below. Then paraphrase it. Use the back of this page if you need extra space.

Quote: _____

_____

_____

_____

Looking at Text

Directions: Read the article below. Answer the questions that follow below and on the next page.

Woman Wins Money with Chocolate Cake
By Crystal Ball

A young woman in Gary, Indiana, is richer today after winning a cash prize of $1,000 in a local cooking contest on Saturday.

Selma Strausser couldn't believe her luck when she heard about the cooking contest that was coming to her hometown. Selma said, "I've always loved to cook, and I knew my chocolate cake might have a good chance of winning the $1,000 prize money. Yes, it's that delicious!"

Selma Strausser's luck and cooking skills paid off. Her chocolate cake recipe was chosen over 50 other entrants. When asked what she planned to do with her prize money, Selma stated, "I plan to take my family on a vacation to the beach. Of course, I'll carry some cake along with us because it makes a great road trip snack!"

Selma Strausser's recipe "takes the cake" this year!

1. What is the heading of the article?

   _____

2. Who is the author of the article?

   _____

3. What does the caption state?

   _____

4. Write one quotation by Selma Strausser.

   _____

   _____

Looking at Text *(cont.)*

Answer each question about the article on the previous page with a complete sentence.

| 5. | An *idiom* is a phrase that says one thing, but it actually means something else entirely. The caption under the picture used the phrase "takes the cake." What does this idiom mean? |

_____

_____

| 6. | How many people did Selma compete against for the prize money? |

_____

_____

| 7. | How much prize money did Selma win with her cake recipe? |

_____

_____

| 8. | In which city and state does the contest take place? |

_____

_____

| 9. | List two publications where an article like the one about Selma and her cake might be published. |

    a. _____

    b. _____

Something Extra: Everyone is good at something. Think of something you do that is worthy of a prize or trophy. On the back of this page, draw a picture of you winning a prize or trophy for what you do best.

Organizing a Report

Directions: Use the outline below to help begin a report on a topic you know a lot about—you! Follow the directions for each section of the outline.

1. List three facts about yourself.

   a. _____

   _____

   b. _____

   _____

   c. _____

   _____

2. Draw a picture of a place you would like to visit.

3. List three words that best describe you.

   a. _____

   b. _____

   c. _____

4. List three goals you would like to accomplish.

   a. _____

   _____

   b. _____

   _____

   c. _____

   _____

Understanding the Passage

Directions: Read the following passage. Circle the correct answer for each question.

Rosa Parks

Rosa Parks lived in Alabama. She grew up in a time when people of different races were often *segregated*. Rosa did not understand why African Americans could not use the same water fountains as other Americans. She did not agree with many of the laws that existed during her lifetime. One day Rosa decided to take a stand against this *injustice*. Rosa Parks would not give up her bus seat to a man who was not African American. The bus driver asked her to move, but she refused. Her bravery was just the beginning of many important events that would change the way people were treated in America. Rosa Parks died in 2005. She is truly an American hero.

1. For what audience do you think this article was written?

    a. a group of students learning about important people during Black History month

    b. a group of people training to be bus drivers

    c. a group of students preparing for a field trip to the post office

2. Why do you think this article was written?

    a. to entertain   **b.** to persuade   **c.** to inform

3. This article is a/an _____.

    a. autobiography   **b.** biography   **c.** poem

4. According to what you learned in the article, Rosa Parks is a _____ .

    a. fictional character   **b.** mythological character   **c.** nonfictional character

5. The word *segregated* means _____.

    a. all together   **b.** separated   **c.** mixed

Decoding Unknown Words

Directions: Use context clues in each sentence and the chart below to help find the meaning of each underlined word. **Hint:** Use a dictionary for help if needed.

Prefix	Meaning
mal	bad
un	not
audio	sound; hear
auto	self
tri	three
pre	before

1. The students went to view the play in the <u>auditorium</u> because the acoustics there were better than in the gymnasium.

   Define: _____

2. When I turn sixteen, I will get my first <u>automobile</u>.

   Define: _____

3. The children were <u>malnourished</u> and needed vitamins and more nutritious meals.

   Define: _____

4. Look at the word's <u>prefix</u> to help find its meaning.

   Define: _____

5. Sometimes she seems so <u>unreasonable</u> to me, and other times she is very understanding.

   Define: _____

6. The photographer used the <u>tripod</u> to hold the camera in place.

   Define: _____

Synonyms and Antonyms

Directions: A *synonym* has the same meaning as another word and an *antonym* has the opposite meaning. Circle the word that is a synonym of the underlined word. Write the antonym for the underlined word on the line.

---

1. My mother's <u>atrocious</u> cooking often had my father buying food for us at a local diner.

   a. wonderful   **b.** lovely   **c.** terrible

   Antonym: _____

---

2. She received <u>accolades</u> for her wondeful performance in the play.

   a. praise   **b.** criticism   **c.** understanding

   Antonym: _____

---

3. The elephant's <u>behemoth</u> size helps one understand why it is considered the gentle giant.

   a. small   **b.** huge   **c.** petite

   Antonym: _____

---

4. The Greek gods and goddesses were <u>immortal</u>; therefore, they could not die.

   a. mortal   **b.** eternal   **c.** human

   Antonym: _____

---

5. There are a <u>plethora</u> of reasons you should stop being angry with your friend.

   a. excess   **b.** few   **c.** little

   Antonym: _____

---

6. His wonderful <u>illustrations</u> added clarity to the project.

   a. words   **b.** paragraphs   **c.** pictures

   Antonym: _____

Knowing the Difference

Directions: Circle the correct word choice and write it on the line provided. Use a dictionary for help if needed.

---

1. My father took me to see the_____ building in Washington, D.C.

   a. capital   **b.** capitol

---

2. I need a box of _____ so I can write letters to my grandmothers.

   a. stationery   **b.** stationary

---

3. She is upset, but I guess I would be, _____.

   a. to   **b.** too

---

4. Sometimes we do not realize how much our actions _____ others.

   a. effect   **b.** affect

---

5. I really like the _____ of our school because she cares about all the children.

   a. principle   **b.** principal

---

6. I want to go _____ tomorrow or the next day.

   a. there   **b.** their

---

7. Do you think _____ time for us to go?

   a. its   **b.** it's

---

8. Everyone can go _____ Robert and Alicia.

   a. except   **b.** accept

Something Extra: On the back of this page, write definitions for the following troublesome word sets: *effect/affect* and *except/accept*.

Context Clues

Directions: Use the context clues in the passage and the Word Bank below to help finish the story. Write the answers on the lines. Use a dictionary for help if needed.

Word Bank			
famished	unsatisfied	joyous	anguish
resolve	dishonesty	feasted	miscreant

The Cat Detective

Being a cat detective is not always easy. Some cases are almost "impawsible" to

solve, but I simply _____ to find the one who is guilty. When people

1

see me chasing mice, I know they think I'm _____ and searching

2

for food, but that is not so. I am on the "tail" of criminals. The mice often take food

from unsuspecting homeowners without leaving payment for what they take. Such

_____ is wrong. That is how I first became a cat detective. I once

3

lived with a man who loved cheddar cheese. Each night he _____

4

on cheese and crackers. If not, he was simply _____.

5

One night he opened his pantry to find his snack missing. If you could only have

seen the _____ on his face; he was so sad and hungry! Of

6

course, I knew who the _____ was, so I tracked the mouse

7

down and returned the man's snack to his pantry. I know what you're thinking, but

I assure you the mouse had not yet taken a bite, nor actually touched anything but

the wrappers. The man was so _____ when he found his

8

food. It was a "purrfect" day in the life of a cat detective!

Point of View

Stories are told from a *point of view*. Two main points of view are first person and third person. In *first person*, the story is seen through the eyes of one person at a time. In *third person*, there is a narrator who can see many different viewpoints in the story.

Examples

I wish you could tell me why you are so upset. I don't understand why you are so upset. (*first person*)

She wished he could tell her why he was so upset. He wished she would leave him alone. (*third person*)

Directions: Read each scenario. Decide if the section is told in first- or third-person point of view. Circle the correct answer.

1. I always wanted a cat. The day my father brought home a kitten for me was one of the best surprises I ever received. I will never forget the big red bow that was tied around my kitten's neck. What a wonderful day it was!

   a. first person   **b.** third person

2. No one can make a better birthday cake than my mother. She uses a secret recipe my grandmother passed down to her. Mother says when I turn 13, she will teach it to me. I cannot wait! The icing on the cake is also very special, but the icing is a recipe from my father's mother. My grandmothers think it is great that my birthday cake has something special from both sides of my family, and so do I.

   a. first person   **b.** third person

3. They couldn't believe what had happened. The storm came racing through with very little warning. They barely had time to get to the storm shelter. Later, they came out and were amazed to discover the storm had miraculously skipped over their home. Their farmhouse was still there. They knew they would never forget this day.

   a. first person   **b.** third person

Something Extra: On the back of this page, write two paragraphs: one in first-person point of view and one in third-person point of view. Label each paragraph as first person or third person.

Your Own Point of View

Autobiographies are written in first-person point of view. The stories are told from one person's perspective, or viewpoint.

Directions: Follow each set of directions and write sections of your own autobiography in first-person point of view.

1. What is the funniest thing that has happened to you?

   _____

   _____

   _____

2. What is the best gift you have ever given or received?

   _____

   _____

   _____

3. Tell about a moment in your life when you have felt proud of an accomplishment.

   _____

   _____

   _____

4. Write about a time you helped someone or did a good deed.

   _____

   _____

   _____

Something Extra: On the back of this page, rewrite one of the above answers in third-person point of view. **Hint:** Pretend you are interviewing someone else who has the same answers you did.

Plot

All fiction stories have a plot. A *plot* is made of several parts: *exposition*, *rising action*, *climax*, *falling action*, and *resolution*.

> **exposition:** introduces characters, setting, etc.
>
> **rising action:** introduces different levels of excitement in the story
>
> **climax:** the most exciting part of the story
>
> **falling action:** the story begins to wind down
>
> **resolution:** most or all questions are resolved

Directions: Read the story below and complete the plot graph on the following page.

Becca's Dilemma

Becca could not find her backpack. It was time to leave for school, and the bus would be arriving any minute. She looked in all the places she could think of but still found no backpack. When she told her mother the problem, her mother started laughing. Becca did not know what was so funny. Becca's mother moved her in front of a mirror and told her to take a look. Becca could not believe it. Her backpack was on her back! No wonder she had not noticed. Her backpack was nearly empty, and it felt just like her coat. Just then the bus arrived, and Becca left the house with her backpack on her back and a smile on her face.

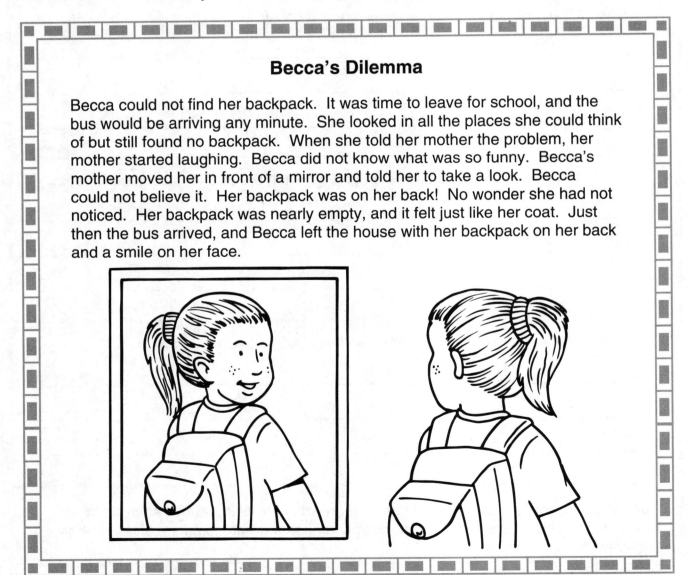

Plot *(cont.)*

Directions: Label the events from the story, "Becca's Dilemma," on the plot graph below.

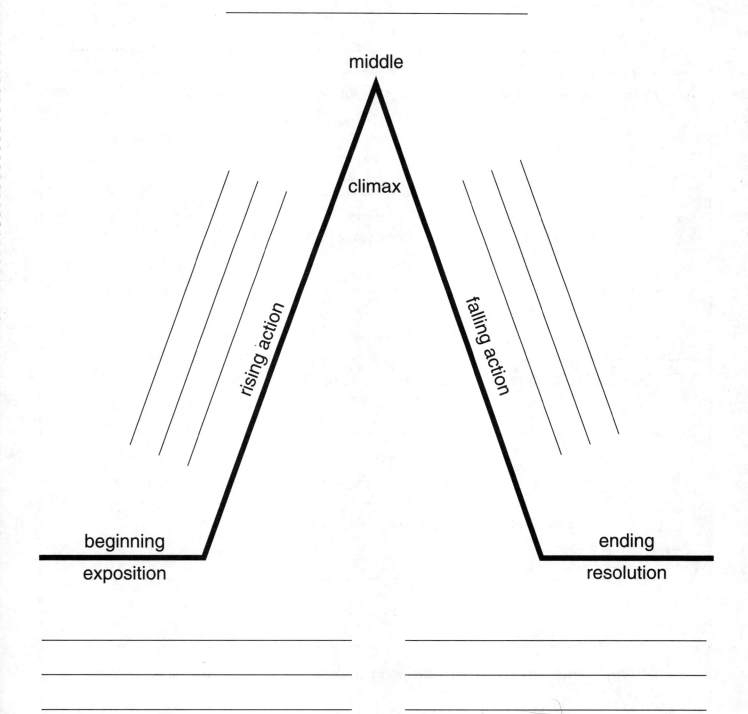

Author's Purpose

Directions: Write a sentence to fit each purpose. **Hint:** When you choose your favorite pet in question 1, use the same animal for the questions that follow.

1. Write a sentence that describes a favorite pet.

_____

_____

2. Write a sentence that gives information about how to take care of a pet.

_____

_____

3. Write a sentence about a pet that is entertaining.

_____

_____

4. Write a sentence that persuades someone to buy a certain pet.

_____

_____

5. Write a sentence that instructs someone how to feed a pet.

_____

_____

Something Extra: On the back of this page, draw a picture of the animal you wrote about for sentence 1.

Cause and Effect

Directions: Write two effects that might result from each cause.

1. A student does not study for a test, and he is not prepared. The student must take the test the next day.

   Possible effects:

   a. _____

   b. _____

2. A child makes an ice-cream cone. He forgets to put the ice cream back in the freezer.

   Possible effects:

   a. _____

   b. _____

3. Some students are playing with a ball in the classroom. The teacher has told them to only play with the ball at outdoor recess.

   Possible effects:

   a. _____

   b. _____

4. Several children are trying out for the talent show. All the students perform well.

   Possible effects:

   a. _____

   b. _____

5. A waitress is new at her job. She has already dropped one tray of food and drops a second tray right on a customer's head.

   Possible effects:

   a. _____

   b. _____

Figurative Language in Literature

Figurative language is used in many types of literature. Some types of figurative language include personification, alliteration, and onomatopoeia.

> **Examples**
>
> **Personification:** giving human characteristics to nonhuman things
> *The sun underline{smiled at me} and warmed my soul.*
>
> **Alliteration:** same consonant sound at the beginning of each word
> *Kelly kicked the kettle off the coffee table.*
>
> **Onomatopoeia:** creating words for sounds
> *The bee buzzed near my ear.*

Directions: Read each sentence. Underline the section of the sentence that uses figurative language. Then circle the correct type of figurative language.

---

1. I tried to resist the chocolate cake but it called to me, so I had to eat a slice.

    a. personification   **b.** alliteration   **c.** onomatopoeia

---

2. When I heard a "hiss" from the snake, I knew I was in trouble.

    a. personification   **b.** alliteration   **c.** onomatopoeia

---

3. The ding dong of the doorbell let me know someone was at the door.

    a. personification   **b.** alliteration   **c.** onomatopoeia

---

4. Does Dan always drive dangerously?

    a. personification   **b.** alliteration   **c.** onomatopoeia

---

5. Why was Warren so worried about his water well?

    a. personification   **b.** alliteration   **c.** onomatopoeia

---

6. The creak of the door was the only indication that someone was hiding upstairs.

    a. personification   **b.** alliteration   **c.** onomatopoeia

---

Metaphors, Similes, and Hyperboles

There are many types of figurative language. *Metaphors*, *similes*, and *hyperboles* are three types of figurative language. They can be used in both poetry and prose.

> **Examples**
>
> **Metaphor:** a comparison between two unlike things
>
> My little <u>sister</u> is a <u>pig</u>; she never cleans her room.
>
> **Simile:** a comparison between two unlike things that uses the words *like* or *as* to make the comparison
>
> My little sister is <u>like a pig</u>; she never cleans her room.
>
> **Hyperbole:** an extreme exaggeration
>
> My little sister is <u>so messy that pigs come to her room to root for food.</u>

Directions: Underline the figurative language in each sentence. Circle the type of figurative language used in each sentence.

1.	He is as mean as a snake.		
	a. metaphor	**b.** simile	**c.** hyperbole

2.	Her ideas are like a breath of fresh air.		
	a. metaphor	**b.** simile	**c.** hyperbole

3.	He is a rock of strength in our time of need.		
	a. metaphor	**b.** simile	**c.** hyperbole

4.	She is so tall it's amazing her head doesn't touch the clouds.		
	a. metaphor	**b.** simile	**c.** hyperbole

5.	You are as strong as an ox.		
	a. metaphor	**b.** simile	**c.** hyperbole

Something Extra: On the back of this page, write your own examples of a metaphor, a simile, and a hyperbole.

Mixed Figurative Language Review

Directions: Use what you know about figurative language to answer the questions below. Use complete sentences.

1. Write a *metaphor* comparing a school day to a circus.

   _____

   _____

2. Write a *simile* comparing summer to a hot stove.

   _____

   _____

3. Write a *hyperbole* exaggerating how loudly someone talks.

   _____

   _____

4. Write a line of *alliteration* repeating the sound of the consonant letter *t*.

   _____

   _____

5. Write an example of *personification* giving the wind human characteristics.

   _____

   _____

6. Write an example of *onomatopoeia* showing the sound a dog makes when barking.

   _____

   _____

Watching Out for Stereotypes

Stereotyping is often used by advertisers and others in the media. *Stereotyping* attributes certain characteristics to an entire group.

> **Examples**
>
> All people with red hair have fiery tempers.
>
> All doctors wear white coats.

Directions: Look at each picture. Determine the stereotype that is used in each one and describe it on the lines provided.

1.

Stereotype:

_____

_____

_____

2.

Stereotype:

_____

_____

_____

3.

Stereotype:

_____

_____

_____

4.

Stereotype:

_____

_____

_____

Do You Think in Stereotypes?

Directions: Draw a picture to represent each item below. Be prepared to share your pictures with the class for a class discussion on stereotypes.

1. Draw a picture of a doctor.	2. Draw a picture of a farmer.

3. Draw a picture of a secretary.

4. Look at the pictures you have drawn. Is there anything about your pictures that might be considered stereotypical? If yes, explain.

_____

_____

_____

_____

Love That Addition

Directions: Color each heart that has the addition problem solved correctly. Correct the answer of each addition problem that is incorrect by writing the correct answer on the line.

1.
```
  12
+ 18
----
  30
```
_____

2.
```
  22
+ 20
----
  54
```
_____

3.
```
  19
+ 12
----
  21
```
_____

4.
```
  89
+ 10
----
  99
```
_____

5.
```
  65
+ 33
----
  88
```
_____

6.
```
  75
+ 21
----
  96
```
_____

7.
```
  52
+ 42
----
  94
```
_____

8.
```
  37
+ 37
----
  64
```
_____

9.
```
  41
+ 17
----
  59
```
_____

10.
```
  65
+ 18
----
  83
```
_____

11.
```
  70
+ 25
----
  95
```
_____

12.
```
  20
+ 11
----
  41
```
_____

13.
```
  39
+ 37
----
  77
```
_____

14.
```
  82
+ 16
----
  98
```
_____

15.
```
  31
+ 19
----
  50
```
_____

What Number Is Needed?

Directions: Solve each addition problem by writing the missing addend on the line.

1. $10 + \underline{\hspace{3em}} = 47$	2. $15 + \underline{\hspace{3em}} = 19$
3. $\underline{\hspace{3em}} + 33 = 52$	4. $56 + \underline{\hspace{3em}} = 62$
5. $\underline{\hspace{3em}} + 72 = 81$	6. $44 + \underline{\hspace{3em}} = 82$
7. $22 + \underline{\hspace{3em}} = 39$	8. $29 + \underline{\hspace{3em}} = 47$
9. $\underline{\hspace{3em}} + 19 = 48$	10. $\underline{\hspace{3em}} + 66 = 72$
11. $81 + \underline{\hspace{3em}} = 90$	12. $17 + \underline{\hspace{3em}} = 61$
13. $19 + \underline{\hspace{3em}} = 34$	14. $\underline{\hspace{3em}} + 34 = 72$
15. $78 + \underline{\hspace{3em}} = 90$	16. $\underline{\hspace{3em}} + 22 = 55$
17. $\underline{\hspace{3em}} + 51 = 69$	18. $37 + \underline{\hspace{3em}} = 61$

Two-Digit Word Problems

Directions: Find the sum to solve each word problem. Show your work.

1.	Caleb brings 22 apples for the students in his class. The next day he brings 22 bananas for the students in his class. How many total snacks did Caleb bring for his classmates? **Show your work:** **Answer:** _____ **snacks**
2.	Helena counted 39 ants carrying bread crumbs from a picnic. Her friend, Autumn, counted 47 more ants also carrying food away from the picnic. How many total ants did Helena and Autumn count? **Show your work:** **Answer:** _____ **ants**
3.	Joshua loves jelly beans. For his birthday, his grandmother gave him 49 blue jelly beans. Joshua already had 19 red jelly beans in a jar at his house. How many total jelly beans does Joshua have? **Show your work:** **Answer:** _____ **jelly beans**
4.	Rita has 32 math problems to complete for homework. Rita also has 12 science problems she must complete. How many total problems does Rita have to complete for school by the next day? **Show your work:** **Answer:** _____ **problems**

Two-Digit Subtraction

Directions: Solve each two-digit subtraction problem.

1. 98 − 43	2. 67 − 21	3. 86 − 29
4. 79 − 39	5. 19 − 12	6. 48 − 39
7. 56 − 28	8. 29 − 17	9. 53 − 48
10. 72 − 34	11. 61 − 35	12. 88 − 77
13. 31 − 27	14. 47 − 29	15. 13 − 11
16. 73 − 38	17. 26 − 17	18. 59 − 52
19. 37 − 21	20. 24 − 16	21. 87 − 69

Subtraction Word Problems

Directions: Find the difference to solve each word problem.

---

1. Roland has $92. He spends $38 at the toy store. After Roland makes his purchase, how much money does he have left?

   Show your work:

   Answer: _____ **dollars**

---

2. Evelyn has collected 79 aluminum cans to recycle. The collection bin is almost full, so Evelyn can only turn in 54 cans. How many remaining cans does Evelyn have?

   Show your work:

   Answer: _____ **cans**

---

3. Charlie saw 23 geese in the pond and watched 17 geese fly away. How many geese remained in the pond?

   Show your work:

   Answer: _____ **geese**

---

4. Juan helped his grandfather pick apples. They gathered 89 apples. Of the apples Juan and his grandfather gathered, 12 had worms in the center. How many apples did not have worms?

   Show your work:

   Answer: _____ **worms**

Mixed Addition and Subtraction with Two-Digit Numbers

Directions: Solve each problem. Circle the problems that are addition problems.

1. 10 + 19	2. 77 − 39	3. 62 − 18
4. 23 + 19	5. 51 + 28	6. 89 − 44
7. 67 − 57	8. 19 − 17	9. 99 − 38
10. 46 + 52	11. 18 + 18	12. 88 − 49
13. 79 + 12	14. 29 − 21	15. 17 + 17
16. 11 + 13	17. 42 + 39	18. 79 − 17
19. 21 − 14	20. 77 + 13	21. 61 − 47

Three-Digit Addition

Directions: Add the three-digit numbers to find each sum.

1. $\begin{array}{r} 722 \\ +\ 231 \\ \hline \end{array}$	**2.** $\begin{array}{r} 456 \\ +\ 333 \\ \hline \end{array}$	**3.** $\begin{array}{r} 581 \\ +\ 190 \\ \hline \end{array}$
4. $\begin{array}{r} 301 \\ +\ 198 \\ \hline \end{array}$	**5.** $\begin{array}{r} 321 \\ +\ 322 \\ \hline \end{array}$	**6.** $\begin{array}{r} 811 \\ +\ 101 \\ \hline \end{array}$
7. $\begin{array}{r} 298 \\ +\ 111 \\ \hline \end{array}$	**8.** $\begin{array}{r} 691 \\ +\ 119 \\ \hline \end{array}$	**9.** $\begin{array}{r} 201 \\ +\ 210 \\ \hline \end{array}$
10. $\begin{array}{r} 410 \\ +\ 333 \\ \hline \end{array}$	**11.** $\begin{array}{r} 561 \\ +\ 198 \\ \hline \end{array}$	**12.** $\begin{array}{r} 871 \\ +\ 112 \\ \hline \end{array}$
13. $\begin{array}{r} 619 \\ +\ 102 \\ \hline \end{array}$	**14.** $\begin{array}{r} 781 \\ +\ 182 \\ \hline \end{array}$	**15.** $\begin{array}{r} 221 \\ +\ 220 \\ \hline \end{array}$
16. $\begin{array}{r} 333 \\ +\ 219 \\ \hline \end{array}$	**17.** $\begin{array}{r} 419 \\ +\ 299 \\ \hline \end{array}$	**18.** $\begin{array}{r} 292 \\ +\ 229 \\ \hline \end{array}$
19. $\begin{array}{r} 557 \\ +\ 198 \\ \hline \end{array}$	**20.** $\begin{array}{r} 108 \\ +\ 292 \\ \hline \end{array}$	**21.** $\begin{array}{r} 677 \\ +\ 339 \\ \hline \end{array}$

Three-Digit Subtraction

Directions: Subtract the three-digit numbers to find each difference.

1. 761 − 298	2. 878 − 333	3. 421 − 129
4. 771 − 381	5. 310 − 229	6. 679 − 401
7. 498 − 377	8. 602 − 202	9. 977 − 199
10. 631 − 334	11. 339 − 229	12. 719 − 541
13. 892 − 700	14. 511 − 322	15. 490 − 402
16. 428 − 209	17. 198 − 189	18. 333 − 241
19. 578 − 339	20. 444 − 319	21. 519 − 289

Three-Digit Addition Word Problems

Directions: Solve each three-digit word problem by finding the sum.

1. There are 397 students at Glascow Elementary School. There are 492 students at Shepherd Elementary School. All students from Glascow Elementary School and Shepherd Elementary School will attend a program at the Chaucer Auditorium. How many total students will attend the program?

   Show your work:

   Answer: _____ **students**

2. There were 276 tickets sold for the dance on Wednesday. On Thursday, 337 tickets were sold for the dance. How many total tickets were sold for the dance?

   Show your work:

   Answer: _____ **tickets**

3. At the volunteer station, 489 volunteers showed up to help the flood victims. The next day, 401 new volunteers showed up to help. How many total volunteers helped during the two days?

   Show your work:

   Answer: _____ **volunteers**

4. At the school carnival, 765 bags of popcorn and 127 bags of cotton candy were sold. How many total bags of treats were sold at the carnival?

   Show your work:

   Answer: _____ **bags of treats**

Mixed Three-Digit Addition and Subtraction

Directions: Solve each word problem. Decide if it is an addition or a subtraction problem and then solve the problem to find the answer.

1. Colleen had 291 trading cards. She gave away 121 of the cards. How many cards did she have left?

   Show your work:

   Answer: _____ **trading cards**

2. There were 721 children who signed up to be in a jump rope competition. On the day of the competition, 111 of the children were unable to attend. How many total children participated in the competition?

   Show your work:

   Answer: _____ **children**

3. The video game store had 821 video games in stock. A new shipment arrived with 197 new games. How many total video games were in the store once the shipment arrived?

   Show your work:

   Answer: _____ **video games**

4. There are 680 gallons of water in the swimming pool. The pool needed more water so 176 more gallons were added to the pool water. How many total gallons of water were in the pool?

   Show your work:

   Answer: _____ **gallons of water**

4-, 5-, and 6-Digit Additon

Directions: Add the numbers to find each sum.

1. 7,992 + 3,391	2. 12,991 + 18,291	3. 8,901 + 1,399
4. 199,761 + 222,102	5. 333,901 + 292,192	6. 19,499 + 22,333
7. 2,390 + 5,190	8. 49,091 + 33,202	9. 7,901 + 2,212
10. 44,777 + 12,871	11. 329,333 + 222,191	12. 6,333 + 2,101
13. 11,889 + 10,711	14. 589,888 + 221,321	15. 29,882 + 22,109
16. 701,000 + 200,100	17. 23,023 + 12,131	18. 11,324 + 10,241
19. 1,111 + 1,101	20. 7,021 + 1,989	21. 56,891 + 22,191

4-, 5-, and 6-Digit Subtraction

Directions: Subtract the numbers to find each difference.

1. 98,371 − 22,390	2. 47,901 − 31,819	3. 3,888 − 1,338
4. 399,210 − 198,001	5. 231,888 − 101,222	6. 24,222 − 12,376
7. 57,810 − 34,123	8. 5,879 − 3,441	9. 44,090 − 21,563
10. 12,989 − 10,222	11. 7,898 − 6,111	12. 9,343 − 4,878
13. 45,222 − 31,090	14. 987,333 − 332,989	15. 20,909 − 13,343
16. 16,454 − 10,132	17. 352,567 − 232,131	18. 11,787 − 10,121
19. 455,321 − 321,123	20. 57,871 − 32,454	21. 8,844 − 3,222

Addition with Estimation

Directions: Round each addend to the nearest hundred. Rewrite the problem on the lines provided, and then find the estimated sum.

> **Example**
>
> ```
>   729        700
> + 166      + 200
>            ─────
>             900
> ```

1.
```
  678          _____
+ 222        + _____
             _____
```

2.
```
  501          _____
+ 341        + _____
             _____
```

3.
```
  291          _____
+ 202        + _____
             _____
```

4.
```
  871          _____
+ 111        + _____
             _____
```

5.
```
  518          _____
+ 329        + _____
             _____
```

6.
```
  347          _____
+ 298        + _____
             _____
```

7.
```
  444          _____
+ 118        + _____
             _____
```

8.
```
  721          _____
+ 378        + _____
             _____
```

9.
```
  638          _____
+ 391        + _____
             _____
```

10.
```
  812          _____
+ 392        + _____
             _____
```

11.
```
  189          _____
+ 101        + _____
             _____
```

12.
```
  555          _____
+ 444        + _____
             _____
```

Mixed Multiplication Practice
with Factors 1–12

Directions: Find the product for each multiplication problem.

1. 7 x 9 = _____	2. 8 x 8 = _____
3. 4 x 12 = _____	4. 2 x 0 = _____
5. 12 x 11 = _____	6. 7 x 3 = _____
7. 5 x 4 = _____	8. 6 x 6 = _____
9. 7 x 8 = _____	10. 11 x 8 = _____
11. 3 x 9 = _____	12. 4 x 11 = _____
13. 5 x 7 = _____	14. 8 x 6 = _____
15. 2 x 6 = _____	16. 3 x 3 = _____
17. 11 x 11 = _____	18. 1 x 9 = _____
19. 0 x 6 = _____	20. 12 x 7 = _____
21. 5 x 9 = _____	22. 4 x 2 = _____
23. 1 x 10 = _____	24. 10 x 10 = _____
25. 5 x 3 = _____	26. 9 x 9 = _____

Calculator Multiplication

Directions: Find the product for each multiplication problem by using a calculator. Write the correct answer in the space provided.

1. 17 x 8 = _____

2. 20 x 8 = _____

3. 45 x 9 = _____

4. 27 x 6 = _____

5. 88 x 2 = _____

6. 16 x 4 = _____

7. 21 x 7 = _____

8. 41 x 8 = _____

9. 76 x 5 = _____

10. 11 x 7 = _____

11. 34 x 4 = _____

12. 59 x 3 = _____

13. 92 x 3 = _____

14. 15 x 9 = _____

15. 45 x 6 = _____

16. 18 x 7 = _____

17. 22 x 9 = _____

18. 39 x 0 = _____

19. 14 x 7 = _____

20. 23 x 8 = _____

21. 77 x 2 = _____

22. 35 x 5 = _____

23. 18 x 9 = _____

24. 21 x 8 = _____

25. 10 x 7 = _____

26. 39 x 4 = _____

Find It

Directions: Look at each circled answer. Circle the multiplication problem that would go with the answer.

1. **a.** 7 x 6 **b.** 7 x 7 (**49**)	**2.** **a.** 4 x 3 **b.** 9 x 2 (**18**)
3. **a.** 11 x 8 **b.** 10 x 8 (**88**)	**4.** **a.** 12 x 12 **b.** 11 x 11 (**144**)
5. **a.** 5 x 12 **b.** 10 x 7 (**60**)	**6.** **a.** 7 x 9 **b.** 8 x 7 (**56**)
7. **a.** 5 x 7 **b.** 9 x 5 (**45**)	**8.** **a.** 3 x 8 **b.** 9 x 3 (**27**)
9. **a.** 7 x 12 **b.** 10 x 8 (**80**)	**10.** **a.** 6 x 6 **b.** 7 x 6 (**36**)
11. **a.** 12 x 8 **b.** 9 x 11 (**99**)	**12.** **a.** 0 x 8 **b.** 4 x 2 (**8**)
13. **a.** 12 x 11 **b.** 10 x 11 (**132**)	**14.** **a.** 4 x 5 **b.** 5 x 5 (**20**)

Practice Makes Perfect

Directions: Find the product for each multiplication problem. Use the example to help you solve each one.

Example

$$\begin{array}{r} 5 \\ 39 \\ \times\ 6 \\ \hline 234 \end{array}$$

6 x 9 = 54 ➜ Write the 4 in the **1s** column. Carry the 5 to the **10s** column.

6 x 3 = 18

18 + 5 = 23 ➜ Write the 3 in the **10s** column. Write the 2 in the **100s** column.

1. $\begin{array}{r} 59 \\ \times\ 2 \\ \hline \end{array}$	**2.** $\begin{array}{r} 37 \\ \times\ 8 \\ \hline \end{array}$	**3.** $\begin{array}{r} 18 \\ \times\ 7 \\ \hline \end{array}$
4. $\begin{array}{r} 29 \\ \times\ 3 \\ \hline \end{array}$	**5.** $\begin{array}{r} 67 \\ \times\ 7 \\ \hline \end{array}$	**6.** $\begin{array}{r} 98 \\ \times\ 4 \\ \hline \end{array}$
7. $\begin{array}{r} 76 \\ \times\ 8 \\ \hline \end{array}$	**8.** $\begin{array}{r} 13 \\ \times\ 9 \\ \hline \end{array}$	**9.** $\begin{array}{r} 33 \\ \times\ 6 \\ \hline \end{array}$
10. $\begin{array}{r} 18 \\ \times\ 5 \\ \hline \end{array}$	**11.** $\begin{array}{r} 66 \\ \times\ 3 \\ \hline \end{array}$	**12.** $\begin{array}{r} 45 \\ \times\ 2 \\ \hline \end{array}$
13. $\begin{array}{r} 65 \\ \times\ 2 \\ \hline \end{array}$	**14.** $\begin{array}{r} 88 \\ \times\ 6 \\ \hline \end{array}$	**15.** $\begin{array}{r} 72 \\ \times\ 2 \\ \hline \end{array}$
16. $\begin{array}{r} 20 \\ \times\ 3 \\ \hline \end{array}$	**17.** $\begin{array}{r} 33 \\ \times\ 9 \\ \hline \end{array}$	**18.** $\begin{array}{r} 16 \\ \times\ 7 \\ \hline \end{array}$

Even Numbers and Multiplication

Directions: Find the product for each multiplication problem. Write the answer inside the balloon. Use a yellow crayon to color only the balloons that have answers that are even numbers.

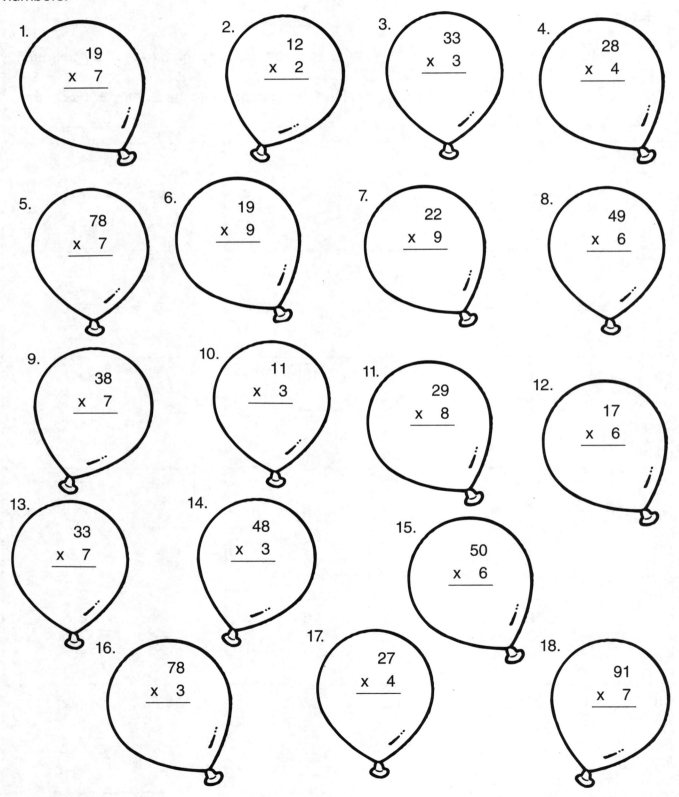

1.
19
x 7

2.
12
x 2

3.
33
x 3

4.
28
x 4

5.
78
x 7

6.
19
x 9

7.
22
x 9

8.
49
x 6

9.
38
x 7

10.
11
x 3

11.
29
x 8

12.
17
x 6

13.
33
x 7

14.
48
x 3

15.
50
x 6

16.
78
x 3

17.
27
x 4

18.
91
x 7

Mastery Multiplication

Directions: Find the product for each multiplication problem. Use the example to help solve each problem. Use a calculator only with your teacher's permission.

Example

```
     987
  x   23
  -------
   2,961
  19,740    Place a zero in the ones place as a place holder.
  -------
  22,701    Add the two columns of numbers to find the answer.
```

1.	2.	3.
238 x 33	671 x 17	912 x 29
4.	**5.**	**6.**
378 x 18	721 x 37	112 x 67
7.	**8.**	**9.**
551 x 78	381 x 51	297 x 43
10.	**11.**	**12.**
821 x 12	576 x 77	390 x 20

More Multiplication Practice

Directions: Use a calculator to find the product for each multiplication problem.

1. 781 x 23 = _____

2. 621 x 11 = _____

3. 652 x 37 = _____

4. 321 x 66 = _____

5. 171 x 44 = _____

6. 404 x 52 = _____

7. 321 x 18 = _____

8. 512 x 12 = _____

9. 661 x 11 = _____

10. 781 x 28 = _____

11. 871 x 10 = _____

12. 555 x 23 = _____

13. 701 x 45 = _____

14. 701 x 56 = _____

15. 802 x 12 = _____

16. 663 x 16 = _____

17. 655 x 28 = _____

18. 704 x 10 = _____

19. 192 x 12 = _____

20. 333 x 72 = _____

21. 984 x 10 = _____

22. 498 x 45 = _____

23. 767 x 13 = _____

24. 881 x 81 = _____

25. 117 x 19 = _____

26. 227 x 17 = _____

Even Divisibility

Some numbers divide evenly with no remainders. When there is no remainder, the dividend is evenly divisible by its divisor.

Example

$$6 \overline{)360} = 60$$

Directions: Find the quotient for each division problem. Be sure to show your work.

1. $2 \overline{)50}$

2. $4 \overline{)480}$

3. $10 \overline{)100}$

4. $20 \overline{)400}$

5. $7 \overline{)280}$

6. $25 \overline{)500}$

7. $9 \overline{)810}$

8. $60 \overline{)3,600}$

9. $8 \overline{)720}$

10. $12 \overline{)1,440}$

11. $20 \overline{)1,600}$

12. $4 \overline{)1,600}$

13. $40 \overline{)8,800}$

14. $15 \overline{)3,000}$

15. $10 \overline{)9,000}$

16. $2 \overline{)160}$

17. $5 \overline{)450}$

18. $4 \overline{)2,800}$

Dividing Whole Numbers

Directions: Divide to find each quotient. Some problems will have remainders. Use a small capital **R** symbol to represent the remainder.

Example

$$52 \overline{)178} \quad \begin{array}{r} 3\ \text{R}22 \\ \hline 178 \\ -156 \\ \hline 22 \end{array}$$

1.
$$20\overline{)198}$$

2.
$$17\overline{)291}$$

3.
$$22\overline{)444}$$

4.
$$33\overline{)898}$$

5.
$$98\overline{)999}$$

6.
$$10\overline{)830}$$

7.
$$54\overline{)678}$$

8.
$$12\overline{)814}$$

9.
$$17\overline{)798}$$

10.
$$39\overline{)981}$$

11.
$$39\overline{)390}$$

12.
$$12\overline{)224}$$

13.
$$67\overline{)889}$$

14.
$$42\overline{)486}$$

15.
$$35\overline{)555}$$

Simply Calculated

Directions: Find the quotient for each division problem. **Hint:** Some problems may have a remainder. Use the **R** symbol to represent the remainder.

> **Example**
>
> 347 ÷ 19 = 18 R5

1. 198 ÷ 18 = _____

2. 389 ÷ 89 = _____

3. 721 ÷ 77 = _____

4. 585 ÷ 72 = _____

5. 298 ÷ 44 = _____

6. 872 ÷ 71 = _____

7. 441 ÷ 13 = _____

8. 561 ÷ 33 = _____

9. 712 ÷ 22 = _____

10. 301 ÷ 11 = _____

11. 822 ÷ 14 = _____

12. 490 ÷ 20 = _____

13. 123 ÷ 17 = _____

14. 501 ÷ 31 = _____

15. 654 ÷ 13 = _____

16. 333 ÷ 15 = _____

17. 229 ÷ 34 = _____

18. 824 ÷ 12 = _____

Adding with Decimals

Directions: Add each decimal to find the sum. Remember to leave the decimal in the same place when adding the numbers.

> **Example**
>
> $$\begin{array}{r} 27.89 \\ +\ 10.10 \\ \hline \end{array}$$
>
> 37.99 (Notice the decimal point did not change places.)

1.
$$\begin{array}{r} 89.12 \\ +\ 10.10 \\ \hline \end{array}$$

2.
$$\begin{array}{r} 16.03 \\ +\ 12.11 \\ \hline \end{array}$$

3.
$$\begin{array}{r} 10.22 \\ +\ 10.22 \\ \hline \end{array}$$

4.
$$\begin{array}{r} 78.43 \\ +\ 17.32 \\ \hline \end{array}$$

5.
$$\begin{array}{r} 52.89 \\ +\ 13.01 \\ \hline \end{array}$$

6.
$$\begin{array}{r} 17.09 \\ +\ 11.99 \\ \hline \end{array}$$

7.
$$\begin{array}{r} 21.45 \\ +\ 12.12 \\ \hline \end{array}$$

8.
$$\begin{array}{r} 49.01 \\ +\ 40.10 \\ \hline \end{array}$$

9.
$$\begin{array}{r} 71.22 \\ +\ 18.09 \\ \hline \end{array}$$

10.
$$\begin{array}{r} 38.71 \\ +\ 12.11 \\ \hline \end{array}$$

11.
$$\begin{array}{r} 48.19 \\ +\ 38.91 \\ \hline \end{array}$$

12.
$$\begin{array}{r} 68.89 \\ +\ 44.01 \\ \hline \end{array}$$

13.
$$\begin{array}{r} 98.01 \\ +\ 21.78 \\ \hline \end{array}$$

14.
$$\begin{array}{r} 22.12 \\ +\ 17.89 \\ \hline \end{array}$$

15.
$$\begin{array}{r} 51.15 \\ +\ 35.12 \\ \hline \end{array}$$

Subtracting Decimals

Directions: Subtract the decimals to find each difference. **Remember:** Do not change the placement of the decimal point when subtracting decimals.

> **Example**
>
> 77.21
> − 22.01
> ———
> 55.20

1.
   12.99
   − 10.10

2.
   78.12
   − 44.10

3.
   89.91
   − 31.02

4.
   69.56
   − 44.12

5.
   19.78
   − 11.87

6.
   20.22
   − 10.11

7.
   72.10
   − 21.09

8.
   29.44
   − 22.11

9.
   44.44
   − 21.03

10.
   14.09
   − 10.90

11.
   70.01
   − 40.33

12.
   51.81
   − 21.08

13.
   98.98
   − 18.02

14.
   67.81
   − 33.07

15.
   18.22
   − 12.10

Multiplying Money

Directions: Multiply each problem to find the total amount of money. Include the dollar sign when writing each answer.

Hint: Place the decimal point by counting the total number of decimal places in the factors. Then count that many places (starting at the right and moving left) in the final answer.

Example

$22.25 (There are 2 decimal places.)

x   3

$66.75 (Move the decimal 2 places to the left.)

1.
$18.97
x   3

2.
$33.90
x   3

3.
$12.25
x   12

4.
$38.44
x   10

5.
$19.83
x   8

6.
$57.90
x   18

7.
$15.22
x   3

8.
$87.20
x   11

9.
$69.90
x   7

10.
$73.10
x   2

11.
$29.92
x   29

12.
$88.44
x   4

Calculator Practice: Multiply Decimals

Directions: Find the product for each multiplication problem. Use a calculator to find each answer.

1. 19.23 x 22 = _____	**2.** 11.98 x 9 = _____
3. 27.2 x 2 = _____	**4.** 10.02 x 4 = _____
5. 22.2 x 8 = _____	**6.** 77.36 x 18 = _____
7. 43.91 x 4 = _____	**8.** 30.8 x 3 = _____
9. 14.14 x 5 = _____	**10.** 77.77 x 50 = _____
11. 49.2 x 9 = _____	**12.** 18.21 x 10 = _____
13. 7.1 x 2 = _____	**14.** 55.3 x 20 = _____
15. 38.18 x 3 = _____	**16.** 70.6 x 18 = _____
17. 40.91 x 7 = _____	**18.** 12.7 x 33 = _____
19. 10.10 x 9 = _____	**20.** 17.7 x 7 = _____
21. 89.9 x 3 = _____	**22.** 12.12 x 11 = _____

Dividing with Decimals

Division involving decimals is easy as long as you remember some simple rules.

Example

$$3 \overline{)\, 7.92} = 2.64$$

—Make sure to write the decimal point of the quotient directly above the decimal point of the dividend.

—When dividing with decimals, also remember to divide the way you would divide whole numbers. The steps are exactly the same.

Directions: Find the quotient for each division problem. Remember to place the decimal in the correct place above the dividend. For each answer, round to the nearest hundredth when necessary.

1. $9 \overline{)\, 27.27}$	2. $6 \overline{)\, 18.36}$
3. $4 \overline{)\, 20.48}$	4. $12 \overline{)\, 24.9}$
5. $7 \overline{)\, 2.19}$	6. $4 \overline{)\, 1.18}$
7. $6 \overline{)\, 7.12}$	8. $3 \overline{)\, 22.66}$
9. $2 \overline{)\, 67.2}$	10. $18 \overline{)\, 80.40}$

Decimals in Word Problems

Directions: Read each word problem. Find the sum.

1. Carole Ann has $7.57 to spend at the fair. Her friend, Rhonda, has $5.50 to spend at the fair. In all, how much money do the girls have to spend at the fair?

   Show your work:

   Answer: _____

2. Chevon has been saving his money for four months. He has saved $97.65. His sister, Lisa, has also been saving her money. Lisa has saved $82.78. Chevon and Lisa both want to buy a video game system. They have decided to combine their money to purchase the system. If Chevon and Lisa combine their money, how much money will they have?

   Show your work:

   Answer: _____

3. The middle school held a fundraiser to raise money for the school's library. The first night, the school made $379.57. On the following night, the school made $422.58. In two nights, how much money did the school raise for the library?

   Show your work:

   Answer: _____

4. Claudia is selling strawberries. She has made $654.50 in one week. Her sister, Rena, is selling jam made from the same strawberry patch. Rena has made $500.25 in the same week. In one week, how much money have the two sisters made from their strawberry business?

   Show your work:

   Answer: _____

Understanding Fractions

A *fraction* is a part of a whole thing. When a fraction is written, the top number is called the *numerator*. The bottom number of the fraction is called the *denominator*. The bottom number, or denominator, tells how many total parts there are. The top number, or numerator, tells how many total parts out of the whole part are represented.

Example

Imagine a pie. If a pie is cut into eight pieces and someone

eats one of the eight pieces, it is represented as the fraction $\frac{1}{8}$.

How many pieces of the pie are left? Seven of the eight pieces, or $\frac{7}{8}$.

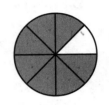

Directions: Look at each picture. Write the fraction for the shaded part of each picture.

1. _____	2. _____
3. _____	4. _____
5. _____	6. _____
7. _____	8. _____
9. _____	10. _____

Finding the Fraction

You will need a crayon for this activity.

Directions: Color the correct number of items needed to equal the fraction given.

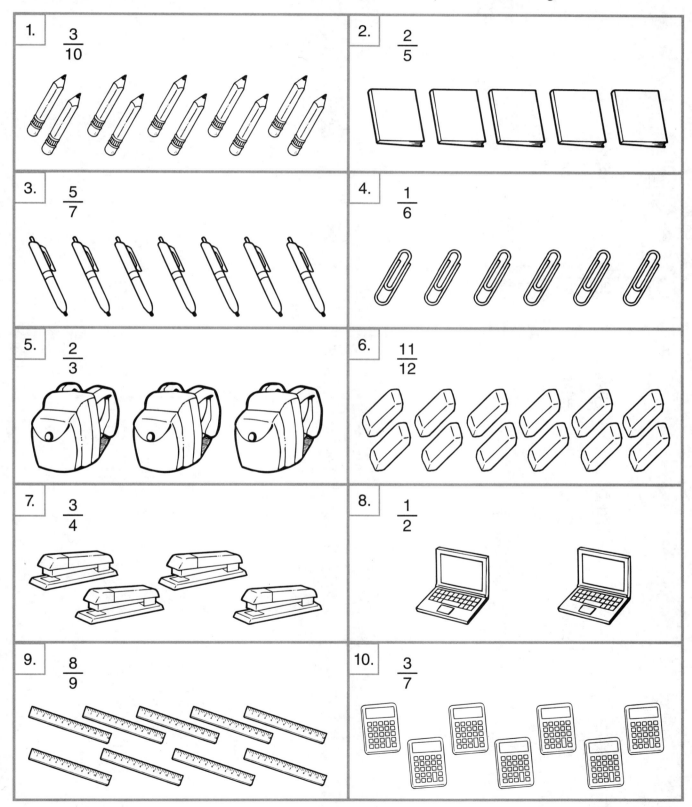

Adding Fractions

Directions: Find the sum of each set of fractions. Write the answer in simplest form.

Example

$$\frac{3}{10} + \frac{2}{10} = \frac{5}{10} \quad \text{or} \quad \frac{1}{2} \text{ (simplest form)}$$

1.

$$\frac{4}{8} + \frac{2}{8} = \underline{\hspace{2cm}}$$

2.

$$\frac{8}{20} + \frac{9}{20} = \underline{\hspace{2cm}}$$

3.

$$\frac{3}{30} + \frac{7}{30} = \underline{\hspace{2cm}}$$

4.

$$\frac{12}{40} + \frac{10}{40} = \underline{\hspace{2cm}}$$

5.

$$\frac{5}{10} + \frac{2}{10} = \underline{\hspace{2cm}}$$

6.

$$\frac{6}{18} + \frac{3}{18} = \underline{\hspace{2cm}}$$

7.

$$\frac{14}{25} + \frac{3}{25} = \underline{\hspace{2cm}}$$

8.

$$\frac{15}{35} + \frac{4}{35} = \underline{\hspace{2cm}}$$

9.

$$\frac{2}{10} + \frac{5}{10} = \underline{\hspace{2cm}}$$

10.

$$\frac{1}{12} + \frac{7}{12} = \underline{\hspace{2cm}}$$

11.

$$\frac{12}{24} + \frac{10}{24} = \underline{\hspace{2cm}}$$

12.

$$\frac{2}{10} + \frac{3}{10} = \underline{\hspace{2cm}}$$

Subtracting Fractions

Directions: Find the difference of each set of fractions. Write the answer in simplest form.

> **Example**
>
> $$\frac{5}{8} - \frac{3}{8} = \frac{2}{8} = \frac{1}{4} \text{ (simplest form)}$$

1.
$$\frac{12}{18} - \frac{4}{18} = \underline{\hspace{3cm}}$$

2.
$$\frac{20}{50} - \frac{3}{50} = \underline{\hspace{3cm}}$$

3.
$$\frac{7}{12} - \frac{5}{12} = \underline{\hspace{3cm}}$$

4.
$$\frac{3}{14} - \frac{1}{14} = \underline{\hspace{3cm}}$$

5.
$$\frac{8}{9} - \frac{2}{9} = \underline{\hspace{3cm}}$$

6.
$$\frac{5}{7} - \frac{2}{7} = \underline{\hspace{3cm}}$$

7.
$$\frac{4}{8} - \frac{1}{8} = \underline{\hspace{3cm}}$$

8.
$$\frac{11}{20} - \frac{6}{20} = \underline{\hspace{3cm}}$$

9.
$$\frac{9}{11} - \frac{3}{11} = \underline{\hspace{3cm}}$$

10.
$$\frac{16}{26} - \frac{4}{26} = \underline{\hspace{3cm}}$$

11.
$$\frac{2}{9} - \frac{1}{9} = \underline{\hspace{3cm}}$$

12.
$$\frac{5}{10} - \frac{3}{10} = \underline{\hspace{3cm}}$$

13.
$$\frac{7}{13} - \frac{2}{13} = \underline{\hspace{3cm}}$$

14.
$$\frac{16}{33} - \frac{10}{33} = \underline{\hspace{3cm}}$$

Working with Improper Fractions

Directions: Write each fraction as a mixed number. Simplify if needed.

> **Example**
>
> $\dfrac{18}{10} = 1\dfrac{8}{10} = 1\dfrac{4}{5}$ (simplest form)

1.

$\dfrac{9}{4} =$ _____

2.

$\dfrac{12}{8} =$ _____

3.

$\dfrac{7}{2} =$ _____

4.

$\dfrac{10}{7} =$ _____

5.

$\dfrac{8}{5} =$ _____

6.

$\dfrac{4}{3} =$ _____

7.

$\dfrac{8}{3} =$ _____

8.

$\dfrac{13}{6} =$ _____

9.

$\dfrac{6}{4} =$ _____

10.

$\dfrac{17}{5} =$ _____

11.

$\dfrac{9}{2} =$ _____

12.

$\dfrac{11}{7} =$ _____

13.

$\dfrac{12}{5} =$ _____

14.

$\dfrac{5}{2} =$ _____

15.

$\dfrac{8}{6} =$ _____

16.

$\dfrac{22}{3} =$ _____

17.

$\dfrac{9}{4} =$ _____

18.

$\dfrac{13}{3} =$ _____

Fractions in Word Problems

Directions: Solve each word problem. Show your work and write each answer on the line. Write each fraction in simplest form.

---

1. Marissa had a pie cut into eight pieces. For lunch, she ate $\frac{1}{8}$ of the pie. For supper, she and her brother ate $\frac{2}{8}$ of the pie. How much of the pie was left? Show your answer in the form of a fraction.

Show your work:

Answer: _____

---

2. There are 28 students in Mrs. Fizer's class. Ten of the 28 students are going on a picnic. What fraction of the students are not attending the picnic? Show your answer in the form of a fraction.

Show your work:

Answer: _____

---

3. There are eight letters in the word *birthday*. What fraction of the letters in the word *birthday* are vowels and not consonants?

Show your work:

Answer: _____

---

4. There are 16 rooms in Carla's house. Carla has cleaned 4 of the 16 rooms. What fraction of the rooms does Carla still need to clean?

Show your work:

Answer: _____

Finding the Perimeter of a Rectangle

When you find the distance around a figure, you are finding the *perimeter* of the object.

You can find the perimeter of an object by adding the length of each side together.

> **Example**
>
> To find the perimeter of a rectangle, use the following formula:
>
> **P** = (l + w) x 2
> **P** = (9 + 2) x 2
> **P** = 11 x 2
> **P** = 22 cm
>
>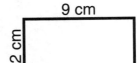

Directions: Find the perimeter of each object. (**Note:** The rectangles are *not* drawn to scale.)

1.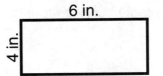

   Perimeter: _____ in.

2.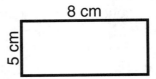

   Perimeter: _____ cm

3.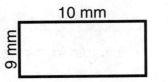

   Perimeter: _____ mm

4.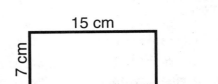

   Perimeter: _____ cm

5.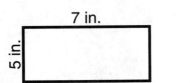

   Perimeter: _____ in.

6.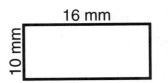

   Perimeter: _____ mm

7.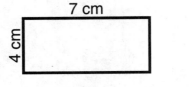

   Perimeter: _____ cm

8.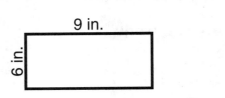

   Perimeter: _____ in.

Finding the Area of Squares and Rectangles

Use the following formula to find the area of a rectangle or square.

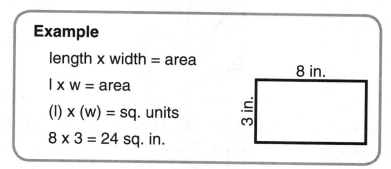

Example

length x width = area

l x w = area

(l) x (w) = sq. units

8 x 3 = 24 sq. in.

8 in.

3 in.

Directions: Find the area of each object. Show your work. (**Note:** The squares and the rectangles are *not* drawn to scale.)

1.
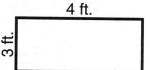
4 ft.

3 ft.

Area: _____ sq. ft.

2.
18 in.

18 in.

Area: _____ sq. in.

3.
3 ft.

2 ft.

Area: _____ sq. ft.

4.
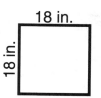
6 ft.

3 ft.

Area: _____ sq. ft.

5.
8 in.

8 in.

Area: _____ sq. in.

6.
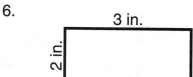
3 in.

2 in.

Area: _____ sq. in.

7.
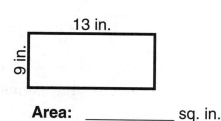
13 in.

9 in.

Area: _____ sq. in.

8.
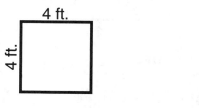
4 ft.

4 ft.

Area: _____ sq. ft.

Triangles: Finding the Area

Use the formula below to find the area of a triangle.

Example

Area = $\frac{1}{2}$ base x height

Area = $\frac{b \times h}{2}$

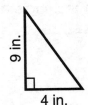

9 in.

4 in.

Area = $\frac{4 \times 9}{2}$ = $\frac{36}{2}$ = 18 sq. in.

Directions: Find the area of each triangle. (**Note:** The triangles are *not* drawn to scale.)

1. 12 in. 8 in. **Area:** _____	**2.** 4 ft. 3 ft. **Area:** _____
3. 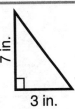 7 in. 3 in. **Area:** _____	**4.** 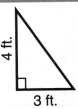 15 cm 10 cm **Area:** _____
5. 17 mm 12 mm **Area:** _____	**6.** 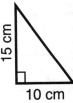 4 in. 2 in. **Area:** _____
7. 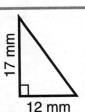 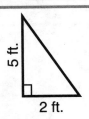 5 ft. 2 ft. **Area:** _____	**8.** 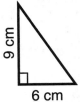 9 cm 6 cm **Area:** _____

Something Extra: On the back of this page, draw your own triangle with measurements clearly written. Then see if a classmate can find the area of that triangle.

Volume – Not Sound

In geometry, the *volume* of an object explains how many cubic units an object contains.

Cubes and rectangular prisms both have volume. The formula for finding the volume of a cube and the volume of a rectangular prism are not the same.

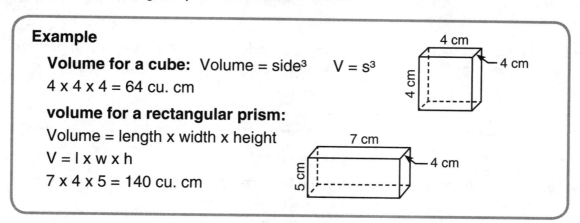

Example

> **Volume for a cube:** Volume = side³   V = s³
> 4 x 4 x 4 = 64 cu. cm
>
> **volume for a rectangular prism:**
> Volume = length x width x height
> V = l x w x h
> 7 x 4 x 5 = 140 cu. cm

Part 1

Directions: Find the volume of each cube. (**Note:** The cubes are *not* drawn to scale.)

1.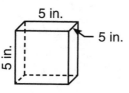

Volume: _____ cu. in.

2.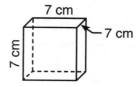

Volume: _____ cu. cm

3.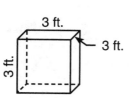

Volume: _____ cu. ft.

4.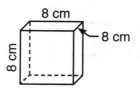

Volume: _____ cu. cm

Part 2

Directions: Find the volume of each rectangular prism.

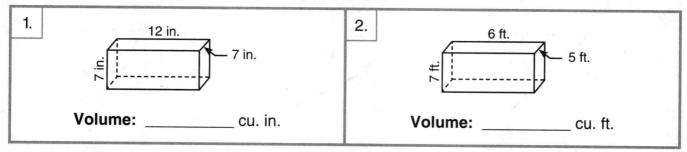

1.

Volume: _____ cu. in.

2.

Volume: _____ cu. ft.

Identifying Angles

You will need a red, a blue, and a yellow crayon for this activity.

When two lines meet, an *angle* is formed. There are three types of angles: *acute*, *right*, and *obtuse*.

acute: angle less than 90 degrees

right: angle exactly 90 degrees

obtuse: angle greater than 90 degrees

Directions: Identify the marked angle of each triangle by using the Color Key below.

Color Key

acute angles: color the triangle **red**

right angles: color the triangle **blue**

obtuse angles: color the triangle **yellow**

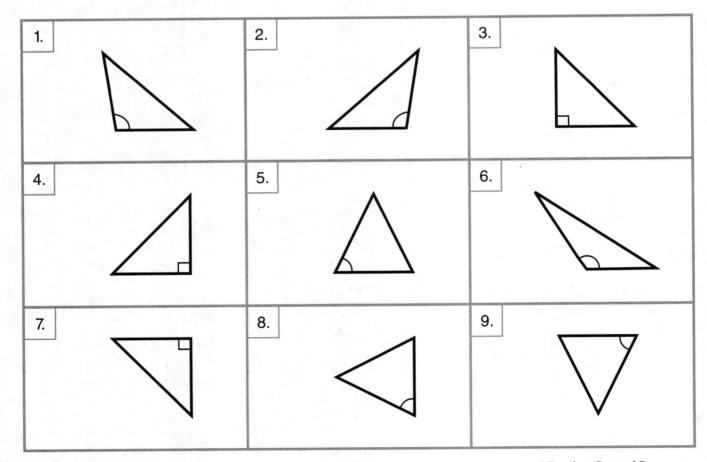

Circumference of Circles

Circumference is the distance around any circle.

Diameter is the distance from one side of the circle to the opposite side of the circle going through the center point of the circle.

To find the circumference of a circle, you must know the diameter of the circle. You can use the radius to find the diameter of the circle. The radius is ½ the diameter. The *radius* is the distance from the center of the circle to any point on the side of the circle.

Example

The formula for finding circumference of a circle is as follows: **C = π x d**

C = 3.14 x d

C = 3.14 x 6

C = 18.84 in.

6 in.

d = 6 inches
r = 3 inches

Directions: Find the circumference of each circle. Round to the nearest tenth as needed. (**Note:** The circles below are *not* drawn to scale.)

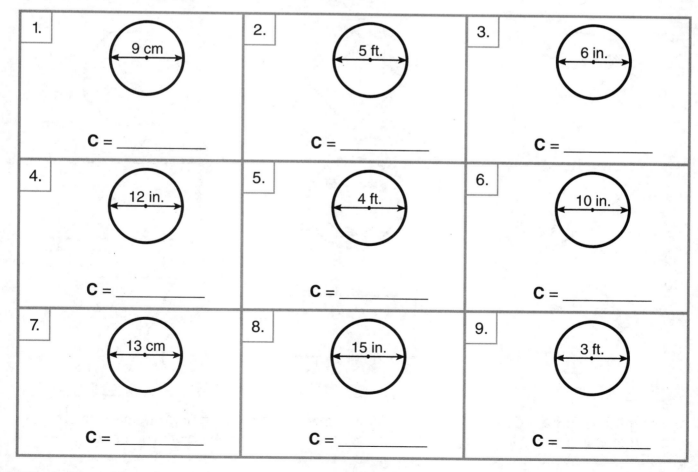

1.   9 cm   C = _____

2.   5 ft.   C = _____

3.   6 in.   C = _____

4.   12 in.   C = _____

5.   4 ft.   C = _____

6.   10 in.   C = _____

7.   13 cm   C = _____

8.   15 in.   C = _____

9.   3 ft.   C = _____

Symmetry

When a shape is *symmetrical*, both sides of the shape are exactly the same. Think about a sheet of copy paper. If that sheet of paper were folded in half, the two parts would overlap and be exactly the same. They would be symmetrical. If the item can be divided evenly into two parts, it is symmetrical.

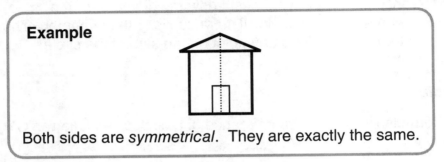

Example

Both sides are *symmetrical*. They are exactly the same.

Directions: Draw a line of symmetry to divide each shape into two identical halves.

1.  2. 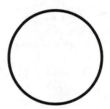 3.

4. 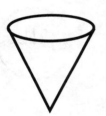 5. 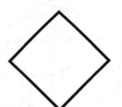 6.

7.  8.  9.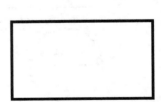

10.  11.  12.

Something Extra: On the back of this page, draw a picture using only objects that are symmetrical. Draw a line of symmetry through the center of each object you draw.

Geometry

Similar and Congruent

You will need a yellow crayon and a red crayon to complete this page.

> **Examples**
>
> Objects that are *similar* have the same shape but not the same size.
> Objects that are *congruent* have the same shape and size.

Directions: Color the picture sets that are *similar* yellow. Color the picture sets that are *congruent* red. Circle the correct answer.

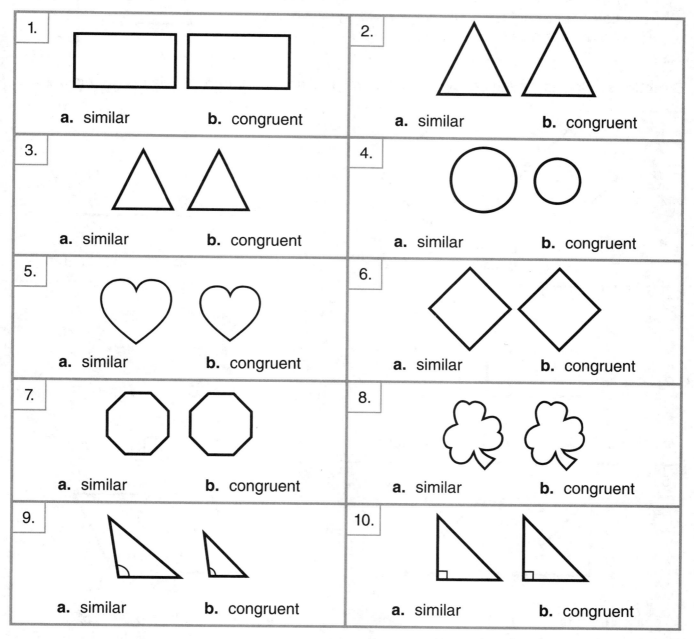

1.
a. similar   b. congruent

2.
a. similar   b. congruent

3.
a. similar   b. congruent

4.
a. similar   b. congruent

5.
a. similar   b. congruent

6.
a. similar   b. congruent

7.
a. similar   b. congruent

8.
a. similar   b. congruent

9.
a. similar   b. congruent

10.
a. similar   b. congruent

Slide, Flip, and Turn

Examples

A *translation* is the movement of a figure on a straight line. A translation is often called a *slide*.

A *reflection* is how a figure appears if it has been flipped. A reflection is also called a *flip*.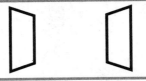

A *rotation* is how a figure is moved or turned from the position it is in—but not by flipping or sliding the figure. This rotation is also called a *turn*.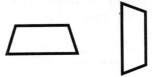

Directions: Decide if each set of pictures shows a *slide, flip,* or *turn*. Circle the correct answer.

1. 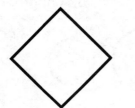 **a.** slide **b.** flip **c.** turn	2.  **a.** slide **b.** flip **c.** turn
3. 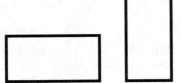 **a.** slide **b.** flip **c.** turn	4.  **a.** slide **b.** flip **c.** turn
5. 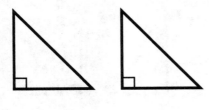 **a.** slide **b.** flip **c.** turn	6. 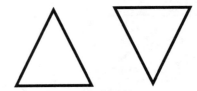 **a.** slide **b.** flip **c.** turn

Working with Lines

There are three types of lines: *parallel, intersecting,* and *perpendicular.*

Examples

parallel: lines that never cross each other

intersecting: lines that cross each other at some point

perpendicular: lines that intersect to form right angles

Directions: Look at each set of lines. Identify the sets as parallel, intersecting, or perpendicular. Circle the correct answer.

1. **a.** parallel **b.** intersecting **c.** perpendicular	**2.** **a.** parallel **b.** intersecting **c.** perpendicular
3. **a.** parallel **b.** intersecting **c.** perpendicular	**4.** **a.** parallel **b.** intersecting **c.** perpendicular
5. **a.** parallel **b.** intersecting **c.** perpendicular	**6.** **a.** parallel **b.** intersecting **c.** perpendicular
7. **a.** parallel **b.** intersecting **c.** perpendicular	**8.** **a.** parallel **b.** intersecting **c.** perpendicular
9. **a.** parallel **b.** intersecting **c.** perpendicular	**10.** **a.** parallel **b.** intersecting **c.** perpendicular

Learning the Terms

Probability is the chance or likelihood something will happen.

Directions: Circle the correct answer for each scenario.

1. What is the probability that a child will find a blue piece of candy in a bag that contains only red pieces of candy?

   a. certain

   b. impossible

   c. likely

   d. unlikely

2. A bag contains one red, one green, and two yellow marbles. What is the probability of pulling out a yellow marble?

   a. certain

   b. impossible

   c. likely

   d. unlikely

3. A child is getting a new puppy. The litter of puppies he is choosing from has three white puppies, two brown puppies, and three puppies that are white and brown. What is the probability he will chose a puppy with black fur?

   a. certain

   b. impossible

   c. likely

   d. unlikely

4. A girl is choosing her jersey for her softball team. The numbers left to choose from are 4, 12, and 18. What is the probability she will choose a jersey with an even number?

   a. certain

   b. impossible

   c. likely

   d. unlikely

Something Extra: On the back of this page, write your own probability problem. List four answer choices. See if a classmate can guess the correct answer.

Probability as a Fraction

Directions: Read the problems. Express each answer as a fraction. Simplify as needed.

1. Carla has a bag of a gum. Five of the pieces are red. Ten of the pieces are blue. Seven of the pieces are green. What is the probability that Carla will pull out a red piece of gum?

   Show your work:

   Answer: _____

2. Sam is playing a game with a spinner. The spinner has the numbers 1–10 written on it. Sam needs to spin any number greater than 6. What is the probability he will spin a number greater than 6?

   Show your work:

   Answer: _____

3. Misty has a deck of cards. There are 52 cards in a deck without the jokers. The deck of cards has 4 different suits: hearts, diamonds, clubs, and spades. What is the probability Misty will draw a diamond from the deck of cards?

   Show your work:

   Answer: _____

4. Charlotte has a bag of marbles. The bag contains nine red marbles, five black marbles, and four multicolored marbles. If she is not looking inside the bag, what is the probability Charlotte will draw a multicolored marble out of the bag?

   Show your work:

   Answer: _____

Working with Simple Equations

Directions: Determine what each variable represents. Then rewrite each problem.

1. $n + 7 = 12$ $n =$ ___ ___ $+ 7 = 12$	**2.** $8 - x = 3$ $x =$ ___ $8 -$ ___ $= 3$
3. $a - 17 = 23$ $a =$ ___ ___ $- 17 = 23$	**4.** $(15 - x) + 3 = 9$ $x =$ ___ $(15 -$ ___$) + 3 = 9$
5. $7 + (n + 3) = 20$ $n =$ ___ $7 + ($___$ + 3) = 20$	**6.** $a + 19 = 33$ $a =$ ___ ___ $+ 19 = 33$
7. $(23 - y) + 7 = 27$ $y =$ ___ $(23 -$ ___$) + 7 = 27$	**8.** $51 - n = 32$ $n =$ ___ $51 -$ ___ $= 32$
9. $z - 47 = 12$ $z =$ ___ ___ $- 47 = 12$	**10.** $18 + y = 44$ $y =$ ___ $18 +$ ___ $= 44$
11. $a + 17 = 28$ $a =$ ___ ___ $+ 17 = 28$	**12.** $98 - b = 77$ $b =$ ___ $98 -$ ___ $= 77$

More Simple Equations

Directions: Circle the answer that correctly completes each equation.

1. $n + 19 = 28$

   a. 8

   b. 9

   c. 47

2. $y - 22 = 7$

   a. 34

   b. 31

   c. 29

3. $(a + 7) - 22 = 25$

   a. 40

   b. 68

   c. 14

4. $x + 11 = 55$

   a. 33

   b. 44

   c. 66

5. $(n - 18) + 9 = 21$

   a. 30

   b. 18

   c. 38

6. $26 + y = 59$

   a. 22

   b. 11

   c. 33

7. $18 - r = 7$

   a. 15

   b. 11

   c. 7

8. $55 = 22 + x$

   a. 33

   b. 22

   c. 35

9. $(7 + y) = 19$

   a. 11

   b. 12

   c. 13

10. $89 - x = 37$

   a. 52

   b. 37

   c. 126

11. $49 = 11 + y$

   a. 60

   b. 40

   c. 38

12. $(22 + a) - 19 = 25$

   a. 41

   b. 22

   c. 19

Equal or Not?

Directions: Look at the symbol in each problem. Circle the answer that correctly completes each problem.

Symbols

$\leq$	is less than or equal to
$<$	is less than
$\geq$	is greater than or equal to
$>$	is greater than
$\neq$	is not equal to

1.	$x > 19$		
	a. 25	**b.** 8	**c.** 12
2.	$y - 3 < 12$		
	a. 12	**b.** 15	**c.** 22
3.	$r \neq 15$		
	a. 15	**b.** 5(3)	**c.** 18
4.	$x \geq 48$		
	a. 18	**b.** 49	**c.** 22
5.	$(7 + n) > 10$		
	a. 2	**b.** 7	**c.** 3
6.	$39 \leq y$		
	a. 59	**b.** 18	**c.** 27
7.	$(x - 18) \neq 2$		
	a. 19	**b.** 20	**c.** 10(2)
8.	$88 + z > 102$		
	a. 10	**b.** 14	**c.** 19
9.	$107 < 96 + x$		
	a. 11	**b.** 12	**c.** 10
10.	$43 > x$		
	a. 53	**b.** 43	**c.** 40

Visual Tools of Math

A *chart* or *graph* is a visual tool to help someone understand information that is given. Charts and graphs are useful tools to see information in a different way. Some people are more visual learners than auditory learners. This means that *seeing* information makes it easier for them to understand than *hearing* information.

Directions: Use the web to answer the questions below.

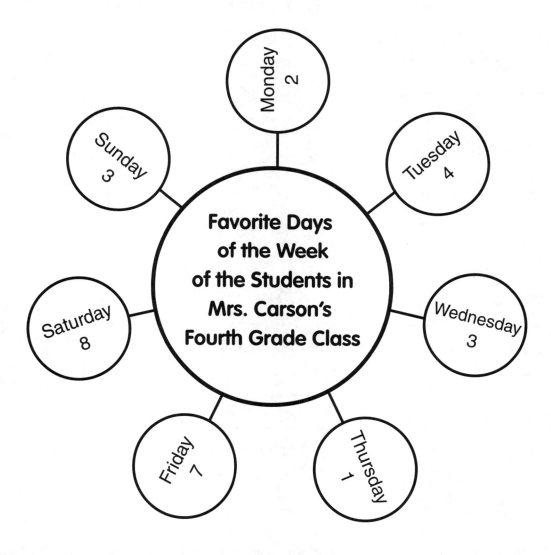

1. How many total students are in Mrs. Carson's class? _____

2. How did you find the answer to question one? _____

3. What day of the week do the students like the best? _____

4. What day of the week do the students like the least? _____

5. Which two days had the same number of votes? _____

6. How many votes did Friday receive? _____

Math

Data and Graphs

Easy Tally Charts

Tally charts are visual representations. A *tally mark*, or line, is made to represent one of each thing that is being counted. After four tally marks, the fifth tally mark is made at a slant to show a set of five.

Examples

Tally marks are frequently used for keeping score in a game.

Team A Жll (= 7)   **Team B** Ж Ж (= 10)

Directions: Use tally marks to answer each question

1.	Show a score of 16.

2.	Show a score of 23.

3.	The girl's team has 18 points. Show the score for the team.

4.	Show the score for the boy's team. The team has 14 points.

5. A baseball team has eight wins and three losses for the season. Show the team's record of wins and losses.

Wins: _____ Losses: _____

6. A soccer team has nine losses and six wins for the season. Show the team's record of wins and losses.

Wins: _____ Losses: _____

126 ©Teacher Created Resources

Bar Graphs

Bar graphs use bars to show information or data. The bars on a bar graph can be drawn horizontally or vertically. Bar graphs have titles so the reader knows what information is being represented.

Directions: Use the bar graph to answer the questions below.

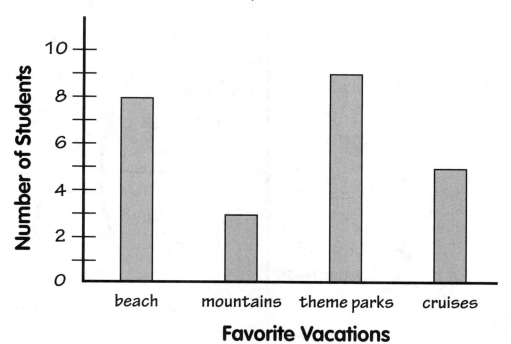

1. What is the title of the bar graph? _____

2. Is this a vertical or horizontal bar graph? _____

3. How many students were asked about what type of vacation they liked? _____

4. Which vacation is the most popular? _____

5. Which vacation is the least popular? _____

6. How many students liked the beach or the mountains? _____

7. How many students liked going on cruises? _____

8. Does this graph give information about the best time of year to take a vacation?

_____ Explain. _____

Pie Charts

Pie charts, or *circle graphs*, show parts of the data and how it relates back to the whole.

Gage's 60-Minute Homework Routine

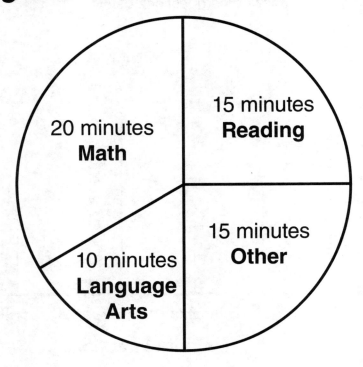

Directions: Use the pie chart to answer the questions.

1. What two names refer to this type of graph? _____

    _____

2. What is the title of the pie chart? _____

3. How many minutes does Gage study math? _____

4. Which subject does Gage study the most? _____

5. Which subject does Gage study the least? _____

6. How many minutes does Gage practice reading each night? _____

7. Why would Gage need 15 minutes each night for "other"? _____

    _____

8. If Gage had 20 minutes of homework in English, from what section would he most likely

    borrow the time he needed?_____

Line Graphs

A *line graph* is another way to visually represent data. It has a *horizontal axis* and a *vertical axis*. A line graph has both horizontal and vertical labels so the reader understands the information that is represented.

> Solomon rescued a puppy from the pound. He wanted to keep track of the puppy's weight gain and decided to make a line graph.

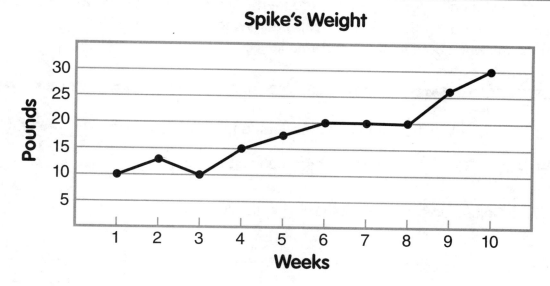

Directions: Use the line graph to answer the questions below.

1. What is the purpose of the line graph titled "Spike's Weight"?

   _____

2. What information is represented by each axis?

   Horizontal _____

   Vertical _____

3. How many weeks does the line graph cover? _____

4. What was Spike's starting weight? _____

   What was the puppy's weight at the end of Week 10? _____

5. Between which two weeks did Spike gain the most weight?

   Week _____ and **Week** _____

6. What happened between Week 6 and Week 8? _____

7. In which week did Spike lose weight? _____

8. How much weight did Spike gain in 10 weeks? _____

Changes Come for Early Americans

Christopher Columbus landed in the Americas in 1492. Columbus mistakenly believed he had landed in the East Indies, so he called the people he met "Indians." These early people were, of course, not Indians, but the term remained. The word was applied to a group of people who really had little in common with one another. There were many different tribes of Native Americans. With the imminent arrival of many Europeans, the lives of these Native Americans was about to change dramatically.

Directions: After reading the paragraph, answer the following questions.

1. What year did Columbus discover the Americas? _____

2. What did Columbus call the people living in the Americas?

   _____

   _____

3. Why do you think the lives of the Native Americans changed once Christopher

   Columbus made his discovery? _____

   _____

4. Think of another title that might be better for the paragraph._____

   _____

5. According to the information given in the paragraph, do you *infer* that all Native Americans lived together or did the tribes live independently from each other?

   _____

   _____

Living from the Land

Native Americans used the resources available to them to meet their basic needs. Food, clothing, and shelter all came from the land. Much of what a tribe used depended on the location.

Tribes that lived near the ocean had a diet of mainly fish. Canoes were carved from nearby trees, and whatever was taken from nature was put to a specific use.

Some tribes were nomads, or wanderers. They did not remain in any one place, but instead followed their food source. Those who lived on the Great Plains followed the buffalo and lived in tepees, so they could easily move from place to place.

Still other tribes were farmers and set up permanent settlements. As one studies the history and culture of each tribe, it is obvious how important the land was to their survival.

Directions: Use the passage above to answer the following questions.

1. Explain at least two ways Native Americans used the land to survive.

   _____

   _____

2. What three basic needs did the Native Americans get from the land?

   _____

3. Define the word *nomad.* _____

4. Why were some tribes nomadic? _____

   _____

5. Explain why the natural resources of the land were so important to the Native Americans.

   _____

   _____

Early Native American Dwellings

Directions: Color the pictures of each Native American dwelling. Then answer the questions below.

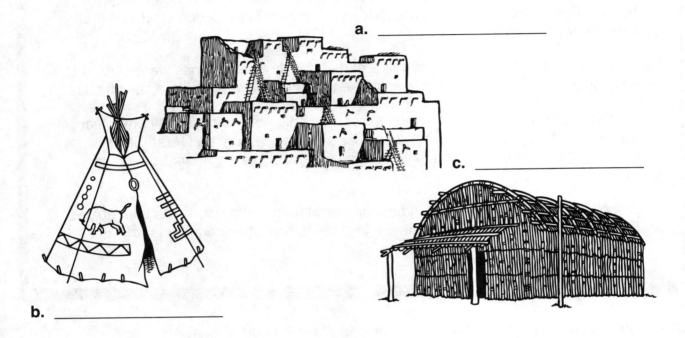

a. _____

c. _____

b. _____

1. Each house belongs to a particular group of Native Americans from a specific region. Write the correct name of the region near each dwelling. Choose from the following: the **Eastern Woodlands**, the **Southwest**, and the **Great Plains**.

2. List one way each dwelling would be practical or helpful to each group of Native Americans.

   a. _____

   _____

   b. _____

   _____

   c. _____

   _____

3. Which dwelling would work best in your area? Explain why you chose this dwelling.

   _____

   _____

Earliest Explorers

Christopher Columbus is known for discovering the Americas, but other explorers played important roles in exploring the New World. Vasco Nunez de Balboa was the first explorer to see the Pacific Ocean. This explorer claimed the great ocean for Spain in 1513.

After Balboa's discovery, others wanted to know just how large the discovery was. Another Spanish explorer and sea captain, Ferdinand Magellan, set out to sail across the ocean. Magellan left Spain around 1519. Although Magellan died before the voyage was completed, one of his ships did find success. The sailors on board were the first people to sail completely around the world, or *circumnavigate* the globe.

Although these early explorers learned many important things about the New World, sadly they would end up spreading war and disease to many of the areas they explored.

Directions: Use the information from the passage to help answer the following questions.

1. Balboa is best known for making this discovery for Spain: _____ .

2. Why would discovery of this ocean be important to early explorers? _____

   _____

3. What was important about Magellan's expedition? _____

   _____

4. What does the word *circumnavigate* mean? _____

   _____

5. What were negative impacts of the early explorers' expeditions?

   _____

   _____

6. If you had lived during the time of these early explorations, would you have wanted to be an explorer? Why or why not?

   _____

   _____

Declaring Independence

Directions: Read each sentence and circle the correct answer. Write the answer on the line provided and reread the sentence.

---

1. The original Thirteen Colonies were part of _____ .

   a. England   **b.** Mexico

---

2. A person who betrays his or her county is known as a _____ .

   a. traitor   **b.** governor

---

3. The Declaration of Independence was written to explain _____ .

   _____

   a. why the colonies wanted to join with Canada

   b. why the colonies wanted to break free from England

---

4. Although many men contributed to the Declaration of Independence,

   _____ is given credit for writing the document.

   a. Benjamin Franklin   **b.** Thomas Jefferson

---

5. The introduction of the Declaration of Independence is referred to as the

   _____ .

   a. body   **b.** preamble

---

6. The Declaration of Independence was approved by the Continental Congress in

   _____ .

   a. 1812   **b.** 1776

Something Extra: Imagine you are being asked to write a declaration of independence from homework or chores. On the back of this page, write a declaration explaining why you should be free from such work.

Understanding the Principles of Democracy

Directions: Answer the questions about American democracy.

1. What does it mean to have the right to life, liberty, and the pursuit of happiness?

   _____

   _____

   _____

2. Why do you think some countries would not want their citizens to have the types of
   rights mentioned in question one? _____

   _____

3. What is something you can do to pursue happiness while still helping those around you?

   _____

   _____

4. Do you think people have a responsibility to help others? Explain. _____

   _____

5. Why is freedom of speech an important part of a democracy? _____

   _____

6. When the Declaration of Independence was first written, did all men and women have
   the same rights? Explain.

   _____

   _____

Changing Times

After the colonies won their independence from England, a new system of government had to be set in place. For a time the new country managed under the Articles of Confederation, but by the late 1780s, the leaders were aware that major changes were needed.

Delegates met in 1787 to revise the Articles of Confederation. However, it did not take them long to realize an entirely new constitution would have to be written. The main plan called for a strong, central government that would share power among three branches: legislative, executive, and judicial. Each branch would have a specific job. The legislative branch would pass laws, the executive branch would carry out laws, and the judicial branch would make sure laws were fair.

Many compromises had to be made before the final Constitution was approved. Delegates had to be willing to give up some demands to get other demands met. After much negotiating, the Constitution was signed in the fall of 1787.

Directions: After reading the passage, answer the following questions.

1. As the colonies became a new country, they first were ruled under the _____ of Confederation.

2. Delegates met in_____ to revise the Articles of Confederation.

3. After the meeting of delegates began, most of them soon realized an entirely new

   _____ would have to be written.

4. The new constitution called for a strong, central _____.

5. The new central government would divide its power between three branches. Name each branch and explain its job.

   _____

   _____

   _____

Researching Important Americans

Certain Americans greatly contributed to establishing the government and ideals that have led America since the late 1700s.

Part 1

Directions: With your teacher's permission, use the Internet, your social studies book, and the library to find out more about the three Americans listed below.

> George Washington   Benjamin Franklin   Thomas Jefferson

Research and find the answers to the following questions about each man. Use a separate sheet of paper for each person listed. Write the name of the person you are writing about at the top of each page.

1. When was he born?

2. How was he involved in the Revolutionary War?

3. Did he have any involvement in writing the Declaration of Independence?

4. Did he have any involvement in writing the Constitution?

5. What is this man best known for in American history?

6. Did this man serve as president of the United States?

Part 2

Directions: After completing Part 1, review your answers to the questions about these three famous Americans. Which one do you most admire? Explain your answer.

_____

_____

_____

_____

_____

_____

_____

New England States

Part 1

Directions: Label each state using its abbreviation. Use the Word Bank for help.

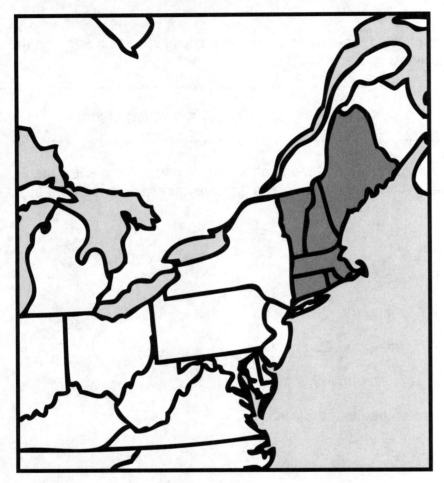

Word Bank

Rhode Island—RI

Massachusetts—MA

Vermont—VT

New Hampshire—NH

Maine—ME

Connecticut—CT

Part 2

Directions: Match each capital to its state. Write the correct capital city on the blank. Then, place a dot on the map to show the location of each state capital.

State Capitals

1. _____ , Rhode Island   **a.** Augusta

2. _____ , Vermont   **b.** Montpelier

3. _____ , Massachusetts   **c.** Concord

4. _____ , Connecticut   **d.** Hartford

5. _____ , Maine   **e.** Providence

6. _____ , New Hampshire   **f.** Boston

Mid-Atlantic States

Part 1

Directions: Label each Mid-Atlantic state using its abbreviation.

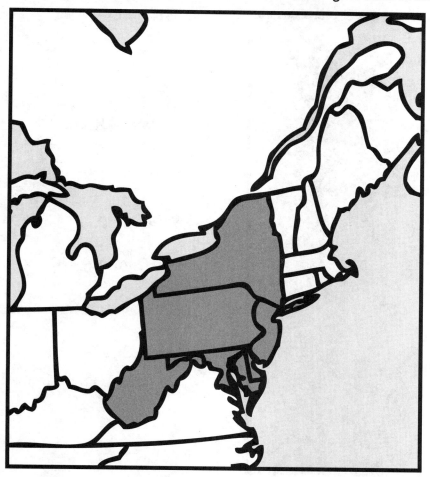

Word Bank

New York—NY

Delaware—DE

New Jersey—NJ

Maryland—MD

Pennsylvania—PA

West Virginia—WV

Part 2

Directions: Match each capital to its state. Write the correct state capital on the blank. Place a dot on the map above to show the location of each state capital.

State Capitals

1. _____ , West Virginia   **a.** Dover

2. _____ , Delaware   **b.** Annapolis

3. _____ , Pennsylvania   **c.** Trenton

4. _____ , Maryland   **d.** Harrisburg

5. _____ , New Jersey   **e.** Albany

6. _____ , New York   **f.** Charleston

Southeastern States

Part 1

Directions: Label each state using its abbreviation. Use the Word Bank for help.

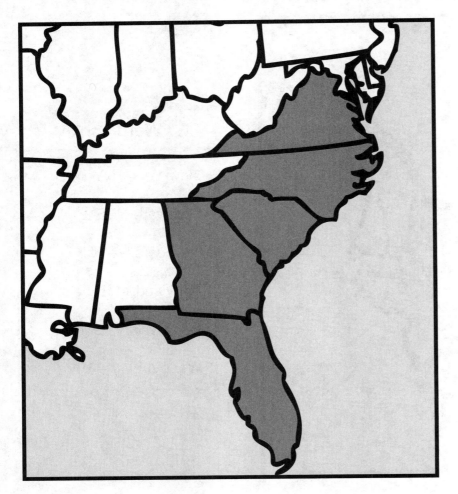

Word Bank

Florida—FL

Georgia—GA

North Carolina—NC

South Carolina—SC

Virginia—VA

Part 2

Directions: Draw a line to match each state to its capital. Place a dot on the map above to show the location of each state capital.

States	**State Capitals**
1. South Carolina	**a.** Raleigh
2. Georgia	**b.** Richmond
3. Florida	**c.** Tallahassee
4. North Carolina	**d.** Columbia
5. Virginia	**e.** Atlanta

Mid-South and Gulf States

Part 1

Directions: Label each state using its abbreviation. Use the Word Bank for help.

Word Bank

Alabama—AL

Louisiana—LA

Kentucky—KY

Missouri—MO

Mississippi—MS

Texas—TX

Tennessee—TN

Arkansas—AR

Part 2

Directions: Draw a line to match each state to its capital. Then, place a dot on the map above to show the location of the state capital.

States	State Capitals
1. Kentucky	a. Jackson
2. Missouri	b. Nashville
3. Tennessee	c. Montgomery
4. Arkansas	d. Baton Rouge
5. Mississippi	e. Little Rock
6. Louisiana	f. Austin
7. Texas	g. Frankfort
8. Alabama	h. Jefferson City

Plains and the Midwestern States

Part 1

Directions: Label each state listed in the Word Bank using its abbreviation.

Word Bank

Iowa—IA	South Dakota—SD	Wisconsin—WI	Ohio—OH
North Dakota—ND	Minnesota—MN	Indiana—IN	Illinois—IL
Nebraska—NE	Kansas—KS	Oklahoma—OK	Michigan—MI

Plains and the Midwestern States (cont.)

Part 2

Directions: Unscramble the name of the capital for each state. The first letter is capitalized.

State	Scrambled Word	Capital
1. Iowa	sDe ionMes	
2. Illinois	flideSirngp	
3. South Dakota	eirPre	
4. Minnesota	tS ulPa	
5. Indiana	ianIndaspoli	
6. Wisconsin	isadMon	
7. Ohio	busmoClu	
8. North Dakota	Bmarkisc	
9. Nebraska	inLcnol	
10. Kansas	opTkea	
11. Oklahoma	lakOamoh ityC	
12. Michigan	ingLsna	

Rocky Mountains and Southwestern States

Part 1

Directions: Use the state abbreviations to label the states on the map. Use the Word Bank to help you.

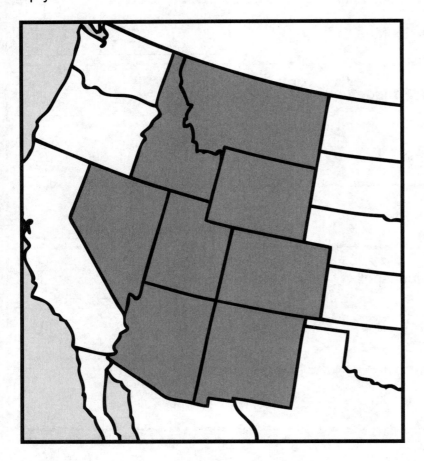

Word Bank

Nevada—NV

Arizona—AZ

Montana—MT

Utah—UT

Idaho—ID

New Mexico—NM

Wyoming—WY

Colorado—CO

Part 2

Directions: The capitals of the states on the map are listed on the chart below. Write the name of the state that goes with each capital. Use the Word Bank to help you.

Capital	State	Capital	State
1. Helena		5. Salt Lake City	
2. Cheyenne		6. Denver	
3. Boise		7. Phoenix	
4. Carson City		8. Santa Fe	

Alaska, Hawaii, and the Pacific Coast States

Part 1

Directions: Label the name of each state. Use the Word Bank for help.

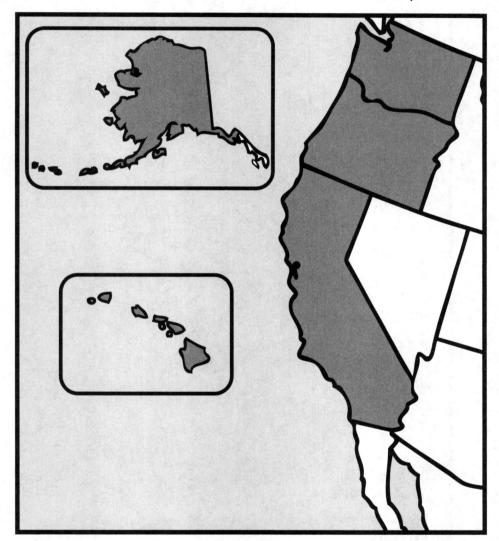

Part 2

Directions: On the map above, find the location of the capital for each labeled state. Draw a star and label each capital. Use the Word Bank.

States		Capitals	
Alaska—AK	California—CA	Honolulu	Sacramento
Hawaii—HI	Oregon—OR	Olympia	Juneau
Washington—WA		Salem	

Looking at the World

Continents and Major Oceans

Looking at the World <small>(cont.)</small>

Directions: Use the map on page 146 to answer the following questions. Use other resources for help, if needed.

1. What is the title of the map?_____

2. Label each continent. How many continents are there? _____

3. Which two continents share a major landmass? _____

   _____

4. On which continent is China located? _____

5. On which continent is Canada located?_____

6. Which ocean is west of the Atlantic Ocean? _____

7. How many oceans are labeled on the map? _____

   List the names of the oceans: _____

   _____

   _____

8. Which continent is located in the southernmost section of the map?

   _____

9. Which continent is closest to North America? _____

10. Italy is part of which continent? **Hint:** The country of Italy is shaped like a boot.

    _____

11. Which continent is a country and a continent? **Hint:** There must be permanent citizens living on the land for it to be considered a country.

    _____

12. Which continent is east of Asia? _____

The Hemispheres

The world is divided into two sections. These two sections are referred to as *hemispheres*, or halves of the globe. The word *hemisphere* comes from the words *hemi*, which means half, and *sphere*, which means ball. The *equator* is the horizontal line that divides Earth into two parts. Of course, there isn't really a line dividing Earth into two sections. This line is an imaginary line. Everything that is located above, or north of, the equator is called the *Northern Hemisphere*. Everything that is located below, or south of, the equator is called the *Southern Hemisphere*.

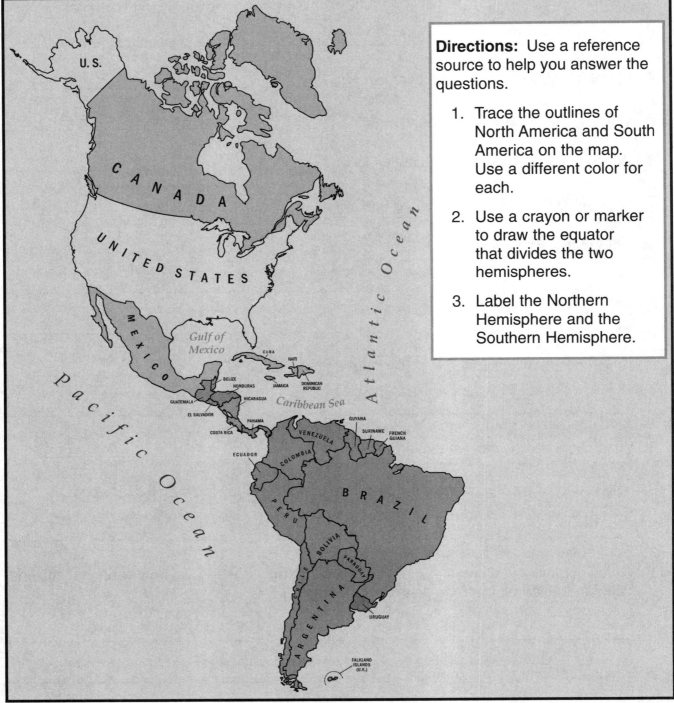

Directions: Use a reference source to help you answer the questions.

1. Trace the outlines of North America and South America on the map. Use a different color for each.

2. Use a crayon or marker to draw the equator that divides the two hemispheres.

3. Label the Northern Hemisphere and the Southern Hemisphere.

All About Heredity

Passing down a trait or traits is called *heredity*. Parents with brown eyes who have children with brown eyes have passed on the trait of brown eyes. Heredity applies to all living things. Both inherited traits and learned behaviors are important for survival.

Instincts are also inherited. Wasps are born knowing how to build nests. This is an *instinct*, or inherited trait, that helps them survive. Of course, all traits are not inherited. If a bird hurts its wings and later has a wing that is not straight, this is a trait developed from its environment.

Some animal behaviors are *learned behaviors*. Have you ever seen a dog do tricks? A dog learns behaviors such as "speaking" and "begging." These behaviors are not hereditary.

Directions: Answer the following questions after reading the passage.

1. Passing down a trait or traits to an offspring is called _____.

2. Heredity applies to all _____.

3. Instincts can also be _____.

4. If a dog learns to speak or sit, this is a _____ behavior.

5. Both inherited traits and learned behaviors are important for _____.

6. List one trait you may have inherited.

   _____

7. List one behavior you have learned.

   _____

8. List one instinct an animal has that helps it survive.

   _____

Inherited Traits and Learned Behaviors

Directions: Read each situation. Then decide if the trait or behavior described is inherited or learned. Circle the correct answer.

1. Jason's mother has blue eyes. Jason has blue eyes just like his mother.

   a. inherited trait   **b.** learned behavior

2. When Cal was four, his older brother taught him to ride his new bicycle. By the time Cal was seven, he had removed his training wheels and could ride his bike without any extra help.

   a. inherited trait   **b.** learned behavior

3. Margaret knows she should not put her elbows on the dinner table. She also knows before she begins eating, she should place her napkin across her lap.

   a. inherited trait   **b.** learned behavior

4. Shay's mother has black hair. Shay's father also has black hair. Shay has black hair just like her mother and father.

   a. inherited trait   **b.** learned behavior

5. Kate has lots of freckles. If she stays out in the sun for a long time her fair skin burns.

   a. inherited trait   **b.** learned behavior0

6. Devon knows coughing can spread germs. Whenever he coughs, he is quick to cover his mouth. He does not want to make anyone else sick.

   a. inherited trait   **b.** learned behavior

Something Extra: On the back of this page, draw a picture of yourself that shows an inherited trait. Describe your inherited trait.

More with Heredity

In the mid-1800s, a German monk named Gregor Mendel began to study how heredity might work. Mendel did experiments using pea plants. After many years of studying these plants, Mendel believed that inherited traits are passed from parents to their biological children.

After many experiments, Mendel learned that some traits are dominant over other traits. The traits that are not dominant are called recessive traits. Recessive traits are often hidden by more dominant traits. For example, brown eyes are usually dominant over blue eyes. So brown is a dominant trait in eye color.

Directions: Read the passage. Circle the correct answer for each question.

1. _____ is credited with discovering how heredity works.

   a. Gregor Mendel

   b. Albert Einstein

2. Mendel believed that _____ traits are passed from parents to their offspring.

   a. learned

   b. inherited

3. Mendel's first experiments were done using _____ .

   a. pea plants

   b. tomato plants

4. Traits that are not dominant are called _____.

   a. recessive traits

   b. instinctive traits

5. Recessive traits can be hidden by _____.

   a. dominant traits

   b. learned behavior

Which Type of Trait?

Crayons are needed for this activity.

Directions: Color the pictures that show inherited traits. Circle the pictures that show learned behaviors.

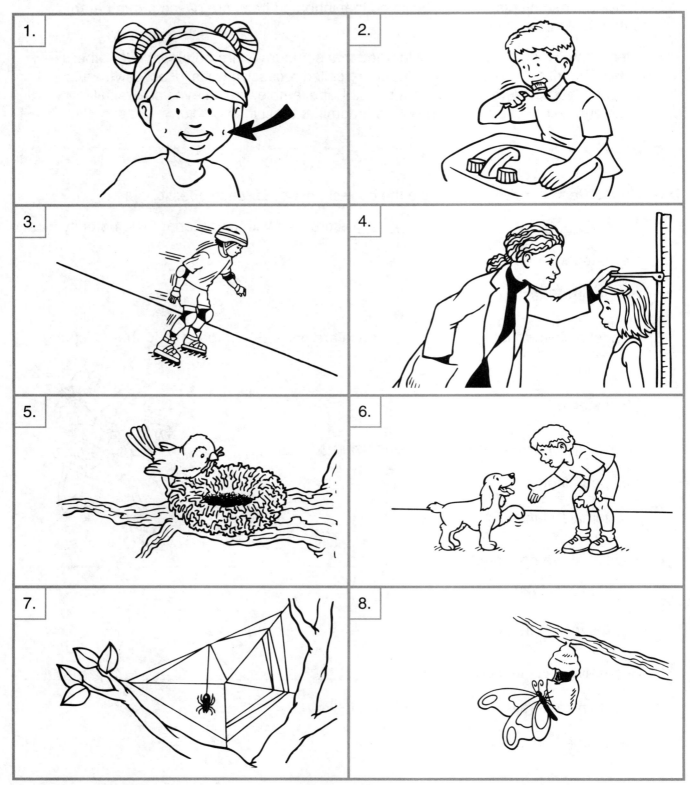

Understanding the Earth

Fossils are used by scientists to help understand Earth's past. A *fossil* is an imprint of the remains of a living thing preserved in parts of the earth such as rocks or dirt. Some examples of fossils include a mosquito trapped and then preserved in sap from a tree or a dinosaur bone buried in the soil. Scientists can study these remains and learn many things about the past.

Of course, not all animals or plants that die turn into fossils. Most organisms decay and are not preserved. However, some organisms become trapped by layers of sediment that preserve part or all of their bodies. This preservation creates the fossils that allow us to compare animals and plants from long ago to those that exist today.

Directions: After reading the passage, respond to each question by writing *true* or *false.*

1. _____ A dinosaur bone discovered in the earth might be an example of a fossil.

2. _____ Only plants or animals preserved in tree sap are considered to be fossils.

3. _____ An imprint of the remains of a living thing that has been preserved is called a fossil.

4. _____ Only the remains of animals can become fossils.

5. _____ Although many fossils have been discovered, scientists can learn very little by studying these ancient artifacts.

6. _____ Most organisms become fossilized.

7. _____ Scientists use fossils to compare organisms that lived long ago to organisms that are living today.

8. _____ Fossils give us no information about what things were like in the past.

Art and Science

You will need crayons to complete this activity.

Directions: Below are rocks that are missing their fossils. Read the description below each rock, then draw the missing fossil.

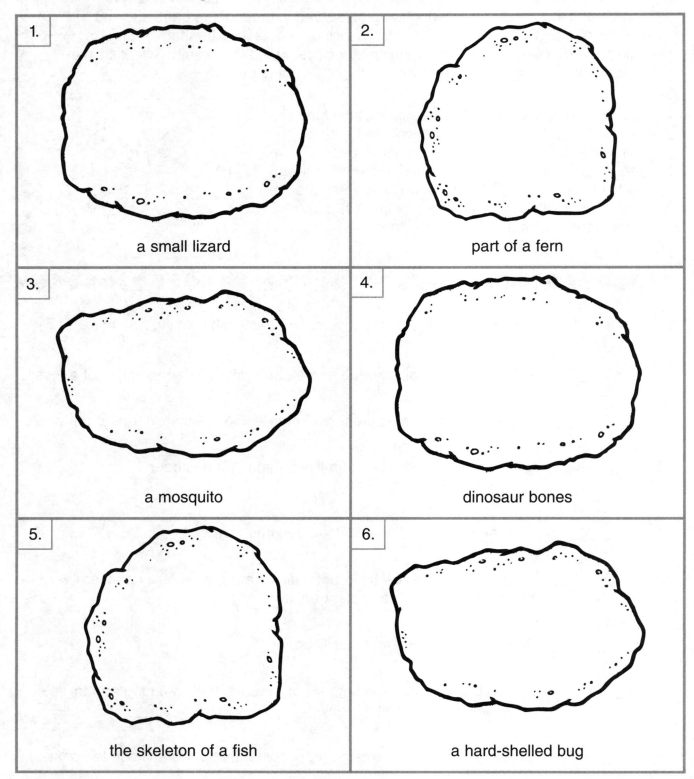

1. a small lizard

2. part of a fern

3. a mosquito

4. dinosaur bones

5. the skeleton of a fish

6. a hard-shelled bug

Planets and the Solar System

Our *solar system* is made up of the star we call the sun and all the planets that orbit this amazing star. The planets also have objects that orbit around them. The moon or moons that orbit each planet are also a part of the solar system.

Asteroids are rocky objects that are in outer space. Asteroids also revolve around the sun, but asteroids are not planets.

The planets are divided into two groups: the inner planets and the outer planets. The *inner planets* are the planets that are closest to the sun. These planets include Mercury, Venus, Earth, and Mars. The planets that are not as close to the sun are called the *outer planets*. The outer planets are Jupiter, Saturn, Uranus, and Neptune.

Directions: After reading the passage, answer the following questions.

1. What is a solar system? _____

   _____

2. Do you live in a solar system? Explain.

   _____

   _____

3. Around what star do all of the planets orbit? _____

4. What is an asteroid?_____

5. Inner planets are planets that are closest to the _____.

6. List the inner planets: _____

7. Planets that are not as close to the sun are called the _____.

8. List the outer planets: _____

   _____

Label the Planets

You will need crayons for this activity.

Directions: Color each planet. Write the name of each planet on the line provided. Use the Word Bank for help if needed.

Word Bank			
Jupiter	Mars	Earth	Saturn
Mercury	Neptune	Uranus	Venus

Something Extra: Research the order of the planets from the sun. Create a mnemonic device, or memory sentence, to help you memorize the names of the planets in the correct order. The first letter of each word in the sentence will represent a planet name. Write your mnemonic on the back of this page.

Science and Writing

Part 1

You know that Earth is one of the planets that orbits the sun, but imagine you have discovered a new planet that orbits the sun. You land on the planet after being in space for many months. You discover the planet is much like Earth, and you can survive on the planet without cumbersome space equipment to help you breathe.

Directions: In your Space Log below, record your findings before you head back to planet Earth. What will you name this new planet? Are there any inhabitants on the planet?

━━ Space Log ━━

_____

_____

_____

_____

_____

_____

_____

_____

_____

_____

Science and Writing *(cont.)*

Part 2

`**Directions:** Using the information from your Space Log on page 157, draw pictures of you on your new planet. Remember to include captions in the round-corner boxes that explain each picture.

All Connected

The environment in which you live is made up of many things. Scientists refer to this as an ecosystem. An *ecosystem* includes all the living and nonliving things in a specific environment. In an ecosystem, there are different populations or species. However, each species might be composed of different types. For example, dogs are a species, but there are many types or varieties of dogs.

All the different populations or species create a community. A *community* includes all the living things in the ecosystem. Everyone and everything in a community is connected. This is one reason why people must help protect ecosystems. When pollution occurs, the delicate balance in the ecosystem is disturbed. It affects food and shelter for different populations. Each negative action causes a reaction in another species. We must realize that in an ecosystem, everything is connected.

Directions: After reading the passage, answer each question by selecting the best answer. Circle the correct answer. Then write the answer on the line and reread the sentence.

1. An environment is made up of _____ .

    a. only one species

    b. many different species

2. An ecosystem includes _____ .

    a. only living things

    b. both living and nonliving things

3. In an ecosystem, population is another word for _____ .

    a. pollution   **b.** species

4. A community is made up of all the _____ .

    a. nonliving things in the environment

    b. living things in the environment

5. In an ecosystem, everything is_____ .

    a. connected   **b.** not connected

Learning About Food Chains

In a *food chain*, energy and nutrients move from one source to another. Food chains are vital to the survival of an ecosystem. All food chains begin with energy from the sun. *Producers* are part of the food chain that use the sun's energy to make their own food. Plants are examples of producers. *Consumers* do not make their own food source. Consumers eat plants or other animals for their energy source.

Animals that eat only plants are known as *herbivores*. Squirrels are an example of a herbivore. Animals that eat only other animals are known as *carnivores*. Lions are an example of a carnivorous animal. Still other animals eat both plants and other animals. These animals are known as *omnivores*. Raccoons are omnivores as are many other animals.

Another important part of the food chain is decomposers and scavengers. *Decomposers* help break down the dead plants and animals on the earth's surface. Termites are important decomposers. *Scavengers* eat leftover animals that are already dead. Vultures are an example of scavengers. Although the job of decomposing may not seem glamorous, it is a vital part of the food chain.

Directions: After reading the passage, answer the following questions.

1. In a food chain, energy and _____ move from one source to another.

2. Food chains are vital to the survival of an _____.

3. Producers use the _____ 's energy to make their own food.

4. _____do not make their own food source.

5. Herbivores are animals that eat only _____.

6. Animals that eat only other animals are known as _____.

7. Animals that eat both plants and other animals are called _____.

8. _____ and _____ help rid the earth of animals and plants that are already dead.

Creating Your Own Food Chain

You will need crayons for this activity.

Directions: Create your own food chain. Remember to label each part of the food chain.

sun

plant: _____

animal: _____

animal: _____

scavenger: _____

decomposer: _____

Photosynthesis

Plants use sunlight to make their food. Sunlight, water, and carbon dioxide are needed for this to occur. After the plant creates sugar, the sugars then go into the veins of the plant and spread throughout the plant to give it energy. This process is called *photosynthesis.*

When sunlight lands on the leaves of the plant, the chlorophyll located there captures the energy from the sunlight. Food is then made in the form of sugars. One waste product of photosynthesis is oxygen. This is how plants give off much needed oxygen into the environment. A waste product for a plant is vital for human life!

Directions: After reading the passage, circle the correct answer for each question. Write the correct answer on the line and reread the sentence.

1. Plants use sunlight to make _____ .

   a. water   **b.** food

2. When plants use sunlight to make food, the process is called

   _____ .

   a. photosynthesis   **b.** energy pyramid

3. For photosynthesis to occur, plants need sunlight, water, and

   _____ .

   a. oxygen   **b.** carbon dioxide

4. Chlorophyll, located in the leaves of the plants, captures energy from

   _____ .

   a. water   **b.** sunlight

What Is Matter?

Everything around you is made of matter. Matter is made of chemical elements. That is why matter is broken into three main groups: *solids*, *gases*, and *liquids*.

Directions: Circle the identity of each state of matter.

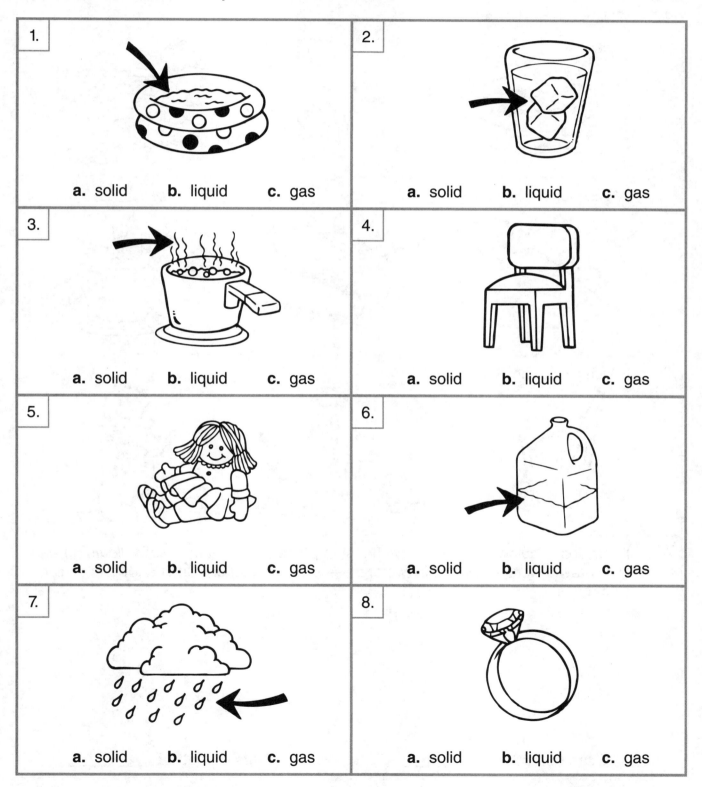

1.

    a. solid   **b.** liquid   **c.** gas

2.

    a. solid   **b.** liquid   **c.** gas

3.

    a. solid   **b.** liquid   **c.** gas

4.

    a. solid   **b.** liquid   **c.** gas

5.

    a. solid   **b.** liquid   **c.** gas

6.

    a. solid   **b.** liquid   **c.** gas

7.

    a. solid   **b.** liquid   **c.** gas

8.

    a. solid   **b.** liquid   **c.** gas

Looking at Water

You will need crayons for this activity.

Directions: Color the picture that correctly answers each question.

1. Which picture shows a *solid*?

2. Which picture shows a *gas*?

3. Which picture shows a *liquid*?

4. In the space below, choose two of the three properties of matter: *solid, liquid,* or *gas.* Now draw a picture of water in two of these states of matter. Color and label your pictures.

State of matter: _____   **State of matter:** _____

Understanding Force and Motion

Motion is a change of position. *Force* is a push or pull between two objects. A force is used to put things into motion.

Although many forces occur because one object touches another, some do not occur this way. For example, magnets can push and pull some objects using magnetic force. These magnets can move other objects made of special materials without ever touching the other object. This is how a compass works. It is pulled by a magnetic force from Earth that makes the compass point north.

Directions: After reading the passage, answer the following questions.

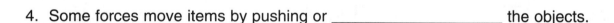

1. A motion is a _____.

2. A force is a push or _____ between two objects.

3. A force can be used to put things into _____.

4. Some forces move items by pushing or _____ the objects.

5. One force that never physically touches another object is a _____ force.

6. Magnets can move objects made of special materials without ever _____ the other object.

7. A compass works using a _____ force from Earth.

8. The magnetic force from Earth causes a compass to always point _____ .

Gravity

Gravity is an important force in our world. Objects fall back to Earth rather than floating into space because of gravity. Gravity also keeps the planets and moons in orbit around the sun.

Sir Isaac Newton studied the effects of gravity on objects. He explained that the mass of the objects and the distance between the objects affects the gravitational force.

Directions: Based on what you have learned about gravity, write a story about a day when there is no gravity on Earth! What would happen on that day? How would things change if there were no gravity? Use the space below to tell about the incredible day without gravity. Illustrate your story on a separate page if you wish.

_____

_____

_____

_____

_____

_____

_____

_____

_____

_____

_____

Tools and Equipment of Scientists

Directions: Draw a line to match each scientific tool to its description.

Tool   **Description**

1. thermometer   **a.** measures time

2. stopwatch   **b.** measures length

3. ruler   **c.** makes a permanent record by taking a picture

4. beaker   **d.** measures temperature

5. scale   **e.** measures volume of a liquid

6. microscope   **f.** measures weight

7. telescope   **g.** allows a close-up look at an object

8. camera   **h.** allows viewing of objects that are far away

Something Extra: On the back of this page, write an example of how a scientist might use each tool.

Answer Key for Fourth Grade

Page 8
1. a 2. b 3. c 4. b 5. b 6. a
Something Extra: Answers will vary.

Page 9
Part 1 and *Part 2:* Answers will vary.
Something Extra: Answers will vary.

Page 10 Answers will vary.

Page 11
1. sandwich, potato
   I ate a ⬭sandwich⬭ for lunch and some ⬭potato⬭ chips, too.
2. there, who's or who is
   ⬭There⬭ is my sister ⬭who's⬭ taking us to the theater.
3. science, experiments
   My favorite class is ⬭science⬭ because we do ⬭experiments⬭
4. Wednesday, February
   I was born on ⬭Wednesday⬭ in the month of ⬭February.⬭
5. nineteen, party
   There were ⬭nineteen⬭ children at the birthday ⬭party.⬭
6. delivery, arrive
   What time do you think our pizza ⬭delivery⬭ will ⬭arrive?⬭

Page 12
1. ? - not a period   2. beach
3. sun - not capitalized
4. ? - not !   5. It's - not Its
6. favorite   7. trying
8. shore   9. is - not are
Something Extra: Answers will vary.

Page 13
Part 1
1. I   2. I   3. E   4. E   5. I
Part 2: Answers will vary.

Page 15
Part 1
1. She, I   2. you, I   3. I, he   4. it, me
5. She, me, I, we
Part 2: Answers will vary.

Page 16
Part 1
Possessive: his, yours, mine, ours, her, their, your, its
Part 2
1. her   2. his   3. their   4. its

Page 17
Part 1
1. gifts   2. men
3. children   4. kids
5. geese   6. oxen
7. boxes   8. books
9. deer   10. pencils

Part 2
1. sock   2. leaf   3. fox   4. student

Page 18
Part 1
1. *singular:* goat, llama, bear, turtle, zebra
   plural: oxen, kittens, geese
2. *singular:* peach, pear, apricot, lemon
   plural: strawberries, apples, grapes, bananas
3. *singular:* muffin, pie, sandwich
   plural: noodles, chips, crackers, beans, cookies
4. *singular:* shirt, sock, jacket, shoe, coat
   plural: belts, sandals
Note: *Pants* can be singular or plural, depending on usage.
Part 2: Answers will vary slightly.
Something Extra: Answers will vary.

Page 19
Answers will vary, but all answers must be capitalized.

Page 20
1. Montana   proper
2. Saturn   proper
3. puppy   common
4. watermelon   common
5. September   proper
6. money   common
7. summer   common
8. toys   common
9. Tuesday   proper
10. kangaroo   common
Something Extra: Answers will vary.

Page 21
1. *subject noun:* Katie
   other nouns: snake, zoo
2. *subject noun:* Allison
   other nouns: swing, tree
3. *subject noun:* Mom
   other nouns: pizza, party
4. *subject noun:* computer
   other nouns: table, library
5. *subject noun:* cat
   other nouns: mouse, clock

Page 22
Part 1
action verbs: sing, walked, yell, ran, talked, played, flew, eat, go
Part 2: Answers will vary slightly.

Page 23
1. jumped—past   2. asked—past
3. types—present   4. called—past
5. takes—present   6. smiles—present
7. makes—present   8. stomped—past
9. sings—present   10. made—past
11. blows—present   12. does—present

Answer Key for Fourth Grade *(cont.)*

Page 24
1. which one   2. which one
3. how many   4. how many
5. what kind   6. how many
7. which one   8. what kind
Something Extra: Answers will vary.

Page 25
1. b   2. a   3. b   4. b
5. a   6. a   7. a   8. b
Something Extra: Answers will vary.

Page 26
Part 1
1. yesterday, here   2. very, there
3. very, happily   4. away, quickly
5. too, slowly
Part 2
2. slower, slowest   3. quicker, quickest
4. softer, softest   5. louder, loudest
6. faster, fastest
Something Extra: Answers will vary.

Page 27 Answers will vary.

Page 28
1. and   2. and   3. nor   4. yet   5. so
6. and   7. or   8. but   9. for   10. but
11. or   12. but   13. or   14. and

Page 29
Part 1
negative words: not, never, hardly, nothing, no, none
Part 2: Answers will vary.

Pages 30–31
Answers will vary, but must all be compound words.
Answers may include the following: sunshine, airplane, football, baseball, superstar, downstairs, butterfly, handyman, spaceship, ladybug, rainbow, dollhouse, sunflower, upstairs, lipgloss, basketball.

Page 32
Part 1
1. isn't   2. should've   3. you'd   4. won't
5. she'll   6. he'd   7. aren't   8. I'd
9. he'll   10. I'm
Part 2
1. I'll   2. she's   3. Isn't
4. He's   5. couldn't

Page 33
1. April   2. Elm Street, Ashland City
3. Pacific Ocean   4. Europe, Australia
5. January   6. Jerry, Betty, Boyte
7. Kelly, Chondra   8. United States

Page 34
1. Don't   2. Today   3. Please   4. It
5. Please   6. The   7. Why   8. I
9. This   10. Watch

Page 35

> 123 Morgan Road
> Hoppy Town, TN 12345
> September 12, 2011
>
> Dear Anne,
>
> How are you? I am doing fine. I hope you will come to see us again soon. It was a lot of fun having you spend the holidays with us. Mom says we may be able to travel to Kentucky soon and see you at your house. If so, we'll call you, of course, before we come.
>
> Yours truly,
> Terry

Page 36
Answers will vary, but must use correct capitalization.
Something Extra: Answers will vary.

Page 37
1. .   2. ?   3. .   4. !   5. !   6. . or !
7. ?   8. .   9. .   10. . or !   11. ?   12. . or !

Page 38
1. Dr. Sanders   2. Mrs. Smith
3. 761 Ellington Dr.   4. 12 in.
5. Washington, D.C.   6. Jan. and Feb.
7. Gen. Washington   8. Mr. Thompson
9. Hwy. 49   10. Cherry Ln.
11. Sept. and Oct.   12. Oak St.
13. Ms. Evans   14. Lt. Brown
15. Toyville Inc.   16. Capt. Hitt
17. Cannon Blvd.   18. Martin Luther King, Jr.
Something Extra: Answers will vary.

Page 39
1. Ave.—Avenue   2. Mr.—Mister
3. Capt.—Captain   4. Inc.—Incorporated
5. Nov.—November   6. Wed.—Wednesday
7. Rd.—Road   8. Jr.—Junior
Something Extra: Answers will vary.

Page 40
1. a   2. b   3. b   4. b   5. b
Something Extra: Answers will vary.

Page 41
1. Dear Thomas, (salutation)
2. Sincerely, (closing)
3. Love always, (closing)
4. Dear Mom, (salutation)
5. Cordially yours, (closing)
6. October 18, 2008 (date)
7. Yours truly, (closing)
8. Dear Linda, (salutation)
9. Tuesday, November 11, 2000 (date)

Page 41 *(cont.)*
10. Always yours, (closing)
11. Dear Grandmother, (salutation)
12. January 1, 1931 (date)

Page 42

> 321 Shadowbrook Lane
> Happy City, New York 54321
> July 19, 2011
>
> Dear Cheyenne,
>
>   I wanted to thank you for letting me come to your house last Friday to ride horses. Sugar is the prettiest horse I have ever seen. She was so gentle. I loved feeding her from the palm of my hand. Thank you, too, for inviting me again next month. I will definitely come back and ride with you.
>
>   Sincerely,
>   *Hannah*

Page 43
Sentences with phrases will vary.
1. the children's toys
2. a girl's doll
3. the house's alarm
4. the geese's feathers
5. a person's problems
6. the students' backpacks

Page 44
Part 1 and *Part 2:* Answers will vary.

Page 45
1. At the wedding, the preacher read from Matthew 3:2.
2. Please bring the following items: glue, scissors, and markers.
3. Dear Madam:
4. Meet me at the store at 7:30.
5. Dear Mr. and Mrs. O'Dell:
6. The ratio on the math worksheet was written as 2:1.
7. Does the movie start at 2:30 or 2:45?
8. Dear Sir:
9. Mrs. Coffman invited the following students to go on the trip: Lisa, Jackson, and Bill.
10. The rules are as follows: no talking and no running.

Page 46
1. "A Little Light"   2. "Silverman and Me"
3. "A Night of Right"   4. "Love Is Funny"
5. "Join the Band"   6. "Love Isn't Fair"
7. "Electric Power"   8. "Creepy Crawlers"
9. "Hip Hop Happy"   10. "Sing Song Sally"
Something Extra: Answers will vary.

Page 47
Answers will vary; however, all answers must contain quotation marks.

Page 48
1. Karla asked, "How long will you be on vacation?"
2. "Tomorrow is going to be a busy day," Penny said.
3. "Will you be able to finish your report on time?" Sam asked.
4. Mom said, "It's time for everyone to get ready for bed."
5. "This movie is too scary!" Alicia exclaimed.
6. "Put that paper in the trash," he said.
7. "What is taking so long?" she asked.
8. "How long will it be before you are ready to go?" Kyle asked.
9. "Watch how I do this," she said.
10. "I have never played baseball," he told his friend.
11. "Stop jumping!" she exclaimed.
12. "I am so hungry," Mary complained.

Page 49
1. a   2. b   3. b   4. a
5. b   6. b   7. a   8. b
Something Extra: Answers will vary.

Page 50
1. "Summer Magic" is a short but wonderful poem.
2. Mr. Rosetta asked the class, "Who is finished with the assignment?"
3. "Why are you so upset?" Jeff asked.
4. I enjoyed the article, "How to Train Your Dog," in Friday's newspaper.
5. My favorite song is "You and Me."
6. "Please be quiet in the library," she said.
7. "Are you going to be late?" he asked.
8. "Look out!" she yelled.

Page 51
1. c   2. d   3. b   4. a   5. a
Something Extra: Answers will vary.

Page 52 Answers will vary.

Page 53
1. b   2. a   3. b   4. c   5. c

Page 54
1. atlas, encyclopedia, glossary, index, Internet
2. almanac, dictionary, magazine, textbook, thesaurus
3. conclusion, paragraph, research, sentence, topic
4. capitalization, grammar, penmanship, punctuation, quotations

Page 55
1. d   2. e   3. f   4. a   5. b   6. c
Something Extra: Answers will vary.

Page 56
1. "Woman Wins Money with Chocolate Cake"
2. Crystal Ball
3. Selma Strausser's recipe "takes the cake"!
4. Answers will vary.

Answer Key for Fourth Grade *(cont.)*

Page 57

5. Answers will vary slightly; it means it is the best.
6. 50   7. $1,000
8. Gary, Indiana   9. Answers will vary.

Something Extra: Answers will vary.

Page 58 Answers will vary.

Page 59

1. a   2. c   3. b   4. c   5. b

Page 60

Answers will vary slightly.

1. a room where the sound is better
2. a vehicle that is mobile or can move by itself (in other words, without the power of a horse or horses)
3. badly nourished or fed
4. something that comes first or at the beginning
5. not reasonable or making sense
6. a device that holds a camera that has three legs or pieces

Page 61

1. c   2. a   3. b   4. b   5. a   6. c

Page 62

1. b 2. a 3. b 4. b 5. b 6. a 7. b 8. a

Something Extra: Answers will vary.

Page 63

1. resolve   2. famished   3. dishonesty
4. feasted   5. unsatisfied   6. anguish
7. miscreant   8. joyous

Page 64

1. a   2. a   3. b

Something Extra: Answers will vary.

Page 65 Answers will vary.

Something Extra: Answers will vary.

Pages 66–67 Answers will vary slightly.

exposition: Becca is introduced as the main character who has a problem.

rising action: Becca looks everywhere for her missing backpack.

climax: Mom shows her the backpack by making Becca look in the mirror.

falling action: Becca realizes the backpack was on her back all along.

resolution: Becca is happy she found her backpack and leaves for the bus.

Page 68 Answers will vary.

Something Extra: Answers will vary.

Page 69 Answers will vary.

Page 70

1. it called to me; a
2. hiss; c
3. ding dong; c

4. Does, Dan, drive, dangerously; b
5. Why, was, Warren, worried, water, well; b
6. creak; c

Page 71

1. b   2. b   3. a   4. c   5. b

Something Extra: Answers will vary.

Page 72 Answers will vary.

Page 73 Answers will vary slightly.

1. a smart person having to wear glasses or a pocket protector and being smart about science
2. a mother being unorganized and not able to look neat
3. a superhero looking perfect and being very strong
4. a teacher has a certain fashion look and an apple in the classroom.

Page 74 Answers will vary.

Page 75

Answers that are correct: 1, 4, 6, 7, 10, 11, 14, 15

2. 42	3. 31	5. 98	8. 74
9. 58	12. 31	13. 76	

Page 76

1. 37	2. 4	3. 19	4. 6
5. 9	6. 38	7. 17	8. 18
9. 29	10. 6	11. 9	12. 44
13. 15	14. 38	15. 12	16. 33
17. 18	18. 24		

Page 77

1. 44	2. 86	3. 68	4. 44

Page 78

1. 55	2. 46	3. 57	4. 40	5. 7
6. 9	7. 28	8. 12	9. 5	10. 38
11. 26	12. 11	13. 4	14. 18	15. 2
16. 35	17. 9	18. 7	19. 16	20. 8
21. 18				

Page 79

1. 54	2. 25	3. 6	4. 77

Page 80

Addition problems: 1, 4, 5, 10, 11, 13, 15, 16, 17, 20

1. 29	2. 38	3. 44	4. 42
5. 79	6. 45	7. 10	8. 2
9. 61	10. 98	11. 36	12. 39
13. 91	14. 8	15. 34	16. 24
17. 81	18. 62	19. 7	20. 90
21. 14			

Page 81

1. 953	2. 789	3. 771	4. 499
5. 643	6. 912	7. 409	8. 810
9. 411	10. 743	11. 759	12. 983
13. 721	14. 963	15. 441	16. 552
17. 718	18. 521	19. 755	20. 400
21. 1,016			

Answer Key for Fourth Grade *(cont.)*

Page 82
1. 463	2. 545	3. 292	4. 390
5. 81	6. 278	7. 121	8. 400
9. 778	10. 297	11. 110	12. 178
13. 192	14. 189	15. 88	16. 219
17. 9	18. 92	19. 239	20. 125
21. 230			

Page 83
1. 889	2. 613	3. 890	4. 892

Page 84
1. 170	2. 610	3. 1,018	4. 856

Page 85
1. 11,383	2. 31,282	3. 10,300
4. 421,863	5. 626,093	6. 41,832
7. 7,580	8. 82,293	9. 10,113
10. 57,648	11. 551,524	12. 8,434
13. 22,600	14. 811,209	15. 51,991
16. 901,100	17. 35,154	18. 21,565
19. 2,212	20. 9,010	21. 79,082

Page 86
1. 75,981	2. 16,082	3. 2,550
4. 201,209	5. 130,666	6. 11,846
7. 23,687	8. 2,438	9. 22,527
10. 2,767	11. 1,787	12. 4,465
13. 14,132	14. 654,344	15. 7,566
16. 6,322	17. 120,436	18. 1,666
19. 134,198	20. 25,417	21. 5,622

Page 87
1. 700 + 200 = 900	2. 500 + 300 = 800
3. 300 + 200 = 500	4. 900 + 100 = 1,000
5. 500 + 300 = 800	6. 300 + 300 = 600
7. 400 + 100 = 500	8. 700 + 400 = 1,100
9. 600 + 400 = 1,000	10. 800 + 400 = 1,200
11. 200 + 100 = 300	12. 600 + 400 = 1,000

Page 88
1. 63	2. 64	3. 48	4. 0
5. 132	6. 21	7. 20	8. 36
9. 56	10. 88	11. 27	12. 44
13. 35	14. 48	15. 12	16. 9
17. 121	18. 9	19. 0	20. 84
21. 45	22. 8	23. 10	24. 100
25. 15	26. 81		

Page 89
1. 136	2. 160	3. 405	4. 162
5. 176	6. 64	7. 147	8. 328
9. 380	10. 77	11. 136	12. 177
13. 276	14. 135	15. 270	16. 126
17. 198	18. 0	19. 98	20. 184
21. 154	22. 175	23. 162	24. 168
25. 70	26. 156		

Page 90
1. b	2. b	3. a	4. a	5. a	6. b	7. b
8. b	9. b	10. a	11. b	12. b	13. a	14. a

Page 91
1. 118	2. 296	3. 126	4. 87
5. 469	6. 392	7. 608	8. 117
9. 198	10. 90	11. 198	12. 90
13. 130	14. 528	15. 144	16. 60
17. 297	18. 112		

Page 92
1. 133	2. 24	3. 99	4. 112
5. 546	6. 171	7. 198	8. 294
9. 266	10. 33	11. 232	12. 102
13. 231	14. 144	15. 300	16. 234
17. 108	18. 637		

problems with even answers: 2, 4, 5, 7, 8, 9, 11, 12, 14, 15, 16, 17

Page 93
1. 7,854	2. 11,407	3. 26,448
4. 6,804	5. 26,677	6. 7,504
7. 42,978	8. 19,431	9. 12,771
10. 9,852	11. 44,352	12. 7,800

Page 94
1. 17,963	2. 6,831	3. 24,124
4. 21,186	5. 7,524	6. 21,008
7. 5,778	8. 6,144	9. 7,271
10. 21,868	11. 8,710	12. 12,765
13. 31,545	14. 39,256	15. 9,624
16. 10,608	17. 18,340	18. 7,040
19. 2,304	20. 23,976	21. 9,840
22. 22,410	23. 9,971	24. 71,361
25. 2,223	26. 3,859	

Page 95
1. 25	2. 120	3. 10	4. 20
5. 40	6. 20	7. 90	8. 60
9. 90	10. 120	11. 80	12. 400
13. 220	14. 200	15. 900	16. 80
17. 90	18. 700		

Page 96
1. 9 R18	2. 17 R2	3. 20 R4
4. 27 R7	5. 10 R19	6. 83
7. 12 R30	8. 67 R10	9. 46 R16
10. 25 R6	11. 10	12. 18 R8
13. 13 R18	14. 11 R24	15. 15 R30

Page 97
1. 11	2. 4 R33	3. 9 R28
4. 8 R9	5. 6 R34	6. 12 R20
7. 33 R12	8. 17	9. 32 R8
10. 27 R4	11. 58 R10	12. 24 R10

Answer Key for Fourth Grade *(cont.)*

Page 97 *(cont.)*
13. 7 R4   14. 16 R5   15. 50 R4
16. 22 R3   17. 6 R25   18. 68 R8

Page 98
1. 99.22   2. 28.14   3. 20.44
4. 95.75   5. 65.90   6. 29.08
7. 33.57   8. 89.11   9. 89.31
10. 50.82   11. 87.10   12. 112.90
13. 119.79 14. 40.01   15. 86.27

Page 99
1. 2.89   2. 34.02   3. 58.89
4. 25.44   5. 7.91   6. 10.11
7. 51.01   8. 7.33   9. 23.41
10. 3.19   11. 29.68   12. 30.73
13. 80.96   14. 34.74   15. 6.12

Page 100
1. $56.91   2. $101.70   3. $147.00
4. $384.40   5. $158.64   6. $1,042.20
7. $45.66   8. $959.20   9. $489.30
10. $146.20 11. $867.68 12. $353.76

Page 101
1. 423.06   2. 107.82   3. 54.4
4. 40.08   5. 177.6   6. 1,392.48
7. 175.64   8. 92.4   9. 70.7
10. 3,888.5 11. 442.8   12. 182.1
13. 14.2   14. 1,106.0 15. 114.54
16. 1,270.8 17. 286.37   18. 419.1
19. 90.9   20. 123.9   21. 269.7
22. 133.32

Page 102
1. 3.03   2. 3.06   3. 5.12   4. 2.08
5. 0.31   6. 0.3   7. 1.19   8. 7.55
9. 33.6   10. 4.47

Page 103
1. $13.07   2. $180.43
3. $802.15   4. $1,154.75

Page 104
1. $\dfrac{1}{6}$ 2. $\dfrac{2}{3}$ 3. $\dfrac{3}{4}$ 4. $\dfrac{5}{6}$ 5. $\dfrac{7}{9}$

6. $\dfrac{1}{3}$ 7. $\dfrac{5}{8}$ 8. $\dfrac{1}{4}$ 9. $\dfrac{5}{12}$ 10. $\dfrac{1}{2}$

Page 105
1. color 3 of the 10 pencils
2. color 2 of the 5 books
3. color 5 of the 7 pens
4. color 1 of the 6 paper clips
5. color 2 of the 3 backpacks
6. color 11 of the 12 erasers
7. color 3 of the 4 staplers

8. color 1 of the 2 laptops
9. color 8 of the 9 rulers
10. color 3 of the 7 calculators

Page 106
1. $\dfrac{3}{4}$ 2. $\dfrac{17}{20}$ 3. $\dfrac{1}{3}$ 4. $\dfrac{11}{20}$ 5. $\dfrac{7}{10}$ 6. $\dfrac{1}{2}$

7. $\dfrac{17}{25}$ 8. $\dfrac{19}{35}$ 9. $\dfrac{7}{10}$ 10. $\dfrac{2}{3}$ 11. $\dfrac{11}{12}$ 12. $\dfrac{1}{2}$

Page 107
1. $\dfrac{4}{9}$ 2. $\dfrac{17}{50}$ 3. $\dfrac{1}{6}$ 4. $\dfrac{1}{7}$ 5. $\dfrac{2}{3}$

6. $\dfrac{3}{7}$ 7. $\dfrac{3}{8}$ 8. $\dfrac{1}{4}$ 9. $\dfrac{6}{11}$ 10. $\dfrac{6}{13}$

11. $\dfrac{1}{9}$ 12. $\dfrac{1}{5}$ 13. $\dfrac{5}{13}$ 14. $\dfrac{2}{11}$

Page 108
1. $2\dfrac{1}{4}$ 2. $1\dfrac{1}{2}$ 3. $3\dfrac{1}{2}$ 4. $1\dfrac{3}{7}$

5. $1\dfrac{3}{5}$ 6. $1\dfrac{1}{3}$ 7. $2\dfrac{2}{3}$ 8. $2\dfrac{1}{6}$

9. $1\dfrac{1}{2}$ 10. $3\dfrac{2}{5}$ 11. $4\dfrac{1}{2}$ 12. $1\dfrac{4}{7}$

13. $2\dfrac{2}{5}$ 14. $2\dfrac{1}{2}$ 15. $1\dfrac{1}{3}$ 16. $7\dfrac{1}{3}$

17. $2\dfrac{1}{4}$ 18. $4\dfrac{1}{3}$

Page 109
1. $\dfrac{5}{8}$ 2. $\dfrac{9}{14}$ 3. $\dfrac{1}{4}$ 4. $\dfrac{3}{4}$

Page 110
1. 20 in.   2. 26 cm   3. 38 mm   4. 44 cm
5. 24 in.   6. 52 mm   7. 22 cm   8. 30 in.

Page 111
1. 12 sq. ft.   2. 324 sq. in.   3. 6 sq. ft.
4. 18 sq. ft.   5. 64 sq. in.   6. 6 sq. in.
7. 117 sq. in.   8. 16 sq. ft.

Page 112
1. 48 sq. in.   2. 6 sq. ft.   3. 10.5 sq. in.
4. 75 sq. cm   5. 102 sq. mm   6. 4 sq. in.
7. 5 sq. ft.   8. 27 sq. cm
Something Extra: Answers will vary.

Answer Key for Fourth Grade *(cont.)*

Page 113

Part 1

1. 125 cu. in.   2. 343 cu. cm
3. 27 cu. ft.   4. 512 cu. cm

Part 2

1. 588 cu. in.   2. 210 cu. ft.

Page 114

1. obtuse (yellow)   2. obtuse (yellow)
3. right (blue)   4. right (blue)
5. acute (red)   6. obtuse (yellow)
7. right (blue)   8. acute (red)
9. acute (red)

Page 115

1. 28.3 cm   2. 15.7 ft.   3. 18.8 in.
4. 37.7 in.   5. 12.6 ft.   6. 31.4 in.
7. 40.8 cm   8. 47.1 in.   9. 9.4 ft.

Page 116

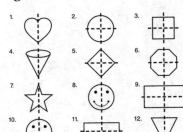

Note: Some shapes can be divided symmetrically in more than one way. Options are given.

Something Extra: Answers will vary.

Page 117

1. b   2. a   3. b   4. a   5. a
6. b   7. b   8. b   9. a   10. b

Page 118

1. a   2. b   3. c   4. b   5. a   6. c

Page 119

1. c   2. a   3. a   4. b   5. c
6. a   7. c   8. c   9. b   10. a

Page 120

1. b   2. c   3. b   4. a

Something Extra: Answers will vary.

Page 121

1. $\dfrac{5}{22}$ 2. $\dfrac{2}{5}$ 3. $\dfrac{1}{4}$ 4. $\dfrac{2}{9}$

Page 122

1. 5   2. 5   3. 40   4. 9   5. 10   6. 14
7. 3   8. 19   9. 59   10. 26   11. 11   12. 21

Page 123

1. b   2. c   3. a   4. b   5. a   6. c
7. b   8. a   9. b   10. a   11. c   12. b

Page 124

1. a   2. a   3. c   4. b   5. b
6. a   7. a   8. c   9. b   10. c

Page 125

1. 28
2. added the numbers in the web
3. Saturday   4. Thursday
5. Wednesday and Sunday   6. 7

Page 126

1. ⅢⅢ ⅢⅢ ⅢⅢ I   2. ⅢⅢ ⅢⅢ ⅢⅢ ⅢⅢ III
3. ⅢⅢ ⅢⅢ ⅢⅢ III   4. ⅢⅢ ⅢⅢ IIII
5. ⅢⅢ III ; III   6. ⅢⅢ I ; ⅢⅢ IIII

Page 127

1. Favorite Vacations
2. vertical   3. 25   4. theme parks
5. mountains   6. 11   7. 5
8. no; Answers will vary slightly. (The graph only tells about the types of vacations students prefer.)

Page 128

1. pie chart or circle graph
2. Gage's 60-Minute Homework Routine
3. 20 minutes
4. math   5. language arts
6. 15 minutes   7. Answers will vary.
8. the section labeled "other"

Options have been suggested.

Page 129

1. Solomon wanted to record Spike's weight gain.
2. Horizontal–Weeks; Vertical–Pounds
3. 10 weeks   4. 10 pounds; 30 pounds
5. 8 and 9   6. Spike's weight stayed the same.
7. Week 3   8. 20 pounds

Page 130

1. 1492
2. He thought he had landed in the East Indies.
3.– 4. Answers will vary.
5. The Native American tribes lived independently of each other.

Page 131

1. Answers will vary.
2. food, clothing, shelter
3. wanderer
4. They followed their food source.
5. Answers will vary.

Page 132

1. a. Southwest
   b. Great Plains
   c. E. Woodlands
2. Answers may vary.
   a. pueblo—good for living where wood is not readily available
   b. log house—good for living where wood is readily available and tribes are not nomadic
   c. tepees—easy to move for nomadic tribes
3. Answers will vary.

Answer Key for Fourth Grade (cont.)

Page 133
1. the Pacific Ocean   2. Answers will vary.
3. The voyage showed that sailors could circumnavigate the globe.
4. It means to sail completely around the world.
5.– 6. Answers will vary.

Page 134
1. a   2. a   3. b   4. b   5. b   6. b
Something Extra: Answers will vary.

Page 135
1.– 5. Answers will vary.
6. no; Answers will vary.

Page 136
1. Articles   2. 1787
3. constitution
4. government
5. legislative–pass laws
   executive–carry out laws
   judicial–make certain laws are fair

Page 137
Part 1 and *Part 2* Answers will vary.

Page 138
Part 1

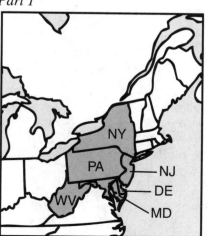

Part 2
1. e
2. b
3. f
4. d
5. a
6. c

Page 139
Part 1

Part 2
1. f
2. a
3. d
4. b
5. c
6. e

Page 140
Part 1

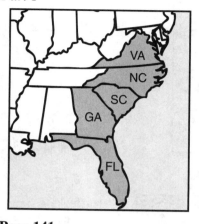

Part 2
1. d
2. e
3. c
4. a
5. b

Page 141
Part 1

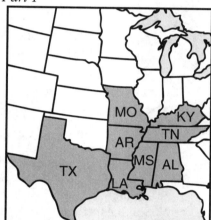

Part 2
1. g
2. h
3. b
4. e
5. a
6. d
7. f
8. c

Page 142
Part 1

Page 143
Part 2
1. Des Moines   2. Springfield   3. Pierre
4. St. Paul   5. Indianapolis   6. Madison
7. Columbus   8. Bismarck   9. Lincoln
10. Topeka   11. Oklahoma City   12. Lansing

Answer Key for Fourth Grade *(cont.)*

Page 144
Part 1

Part 2
1. Montana
2. Wyoming
3. Idaho
4. Nevada
5. Utah
6. Colorado
7. Arizona
8. New Mexico

Page 145
Part 1

Part 2
1. Alaska-Juneau
2. Hawaii-Honoulu
3. Washington-Olympia
4. California-Sacramento
5. Oregon-Salem

Page 147
1. Continents and Major Oceans
2. seven
3. Europe and Asia
4. Asia
5. North America
6. Pacific Ocean
7. three; Pacific, Atlantic, Indian
8. Antarctica
9. South America
10. Europe
11. Australia
12. North America

Page 148

Page 149
1. heredity
2. living things
3. inherited
4. learned
5. survival
6. Answers will vary.
7. Answers will vary.
8. Answers will vary.

Page 150
1. a   2. b   3. b
4. a   5. a   6. b

Something Extra: Check drawings.

Page 151
1. a   2. b   3. a
4. a   5. a

Page 152
Inherited traits: 1, 4, 5, 7, 8
Learned behaviors: 2, 3, 6

Page 153
1. true   2. false   3. true   4. false
5. false   6. false   7. true   8. false

Page 154
Answers will vary, but drawings should resemble descriptions given.

Page 155
1. The solar system is the sun and all the planets that orbit the star, as well as the moons of the planets and the asteroids in the orbit.
2. yes; Answers will vary.   3. the sun
4. An asteroid is a rocky object in space that orbits the sun but is not a planet.
5. sun   6. Mercury, Venus, Earth, Mars
7. outer planets
8. Jupiter, Saturn, Uranus, Neptune

Page 156

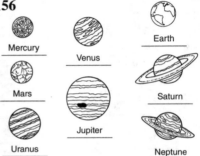

Something Extra: Answers will vary. (MVEMJSUN)

Page 157   *Part 1:* Answers will vary.

Page 158   *Part 2:* Illustrations will vary.

Page 159
1. b   2. b   3. b   4. b   5. a

Page 160
1. nutrients   2. ecosystem   3. sun
4. Consumers   5. plants   6. carnivores
7. omnivores   8. Decomposers and scavengers

Page 161   Answers will vary.

Page 162
1. b   2. a   3. b   4. b

Page 163
1. b   2. a   3. c   4. a
5. a   6. b   7. b   8. a

Page 164
1. solid: ice cubes   2. gas: steam
3. liquid: water   4. Answers will vary.

Page 165
1. change of position
2. pull   3. motion   4. pulling
5. magnetic   6. touching
7. magnetic   8. north

Page 166   Answers will vary.

Page 167
1. d   2. a   3. b   4. e
5. f   6. g   7. h   8. c

Something Extra: Answers will vary.

Bonus Section

This section offers a jump start
for fifth-grade skills in
language arts and math for
those fourth-grade students
who are ready to move ahead.

Working with Quotation Marks

Quotation marks go around a person's exact words. Sometimes a person's words get interrupted. When this happens, the quotation marks start again when the person begins speaking again.

> **Examples**
>
> "Going scuba diving in Hawaii," mused Mike, "would be the perfect vacation."
>
> "Do you," Shondra asked, "think Zander will ask me to the dance?"

Directions: Add quotation marks to each quotation.

1. I wish, Tom said, I could go with you.

2. Do you think, Melinda asked, this is the right one?

3. Maybe tomorrow, Jada said, we'll finally learn the answer.

4. I believe, Mrs. Sanders said, you need to be more careful when writing your answers.

5. Have you ever, asked Margaret, been to Europe?

6. Maybe, Mom said, you can invite some of your friends over next Friday.

7. Something special, said Mia's father, is going to happen on your birthday.

8. Why, asked Kate, does it always seem to rain on the weekends?

9. If you ever get to Boston, Tina said, be sure to visit me.

10. You, Andrea said, are my best friend.

Something Extra: Write an interrupted quotation on the lines below. Don't forget your quotation marks!

_____

_____

Which Is the One?

Directions: Some words sound the same but have different spellings depending on their meaning. Each sentence below contains one word that is used incorrectly. Find the word, circle it, and write the correct word on the line.

1.	Who's turn is it to feed the cat?
	Correct word: _____

2.	I tried to give her a complement on her great work, but she didn't hear me.
	Correct word: _____

3.	Please be sure to site your sources for your research paper.
	Correct word: _____

4.	Many of the skilled emmigrants easily found work when they arrived at their new homes.
	Correct word: _____

5.	They ate allot of pizza at the party.
	Correct word: _____

6.	I thought she was already to go, but she needed a few more minutes.
	Correct word: _____

7.	He took a deep breathe and then dove to the bottom of the pool.
	Correct word: _____

8.	He lead us through the woods and back to our camper.
	Correct word: _____

9.	If you loose the game tomorrow, you don't get to go to the tournaments.
	Correct word: _____

10.	We were glad when the heavy rain past and the sun came out.
	Correct word: _____

Working with Helping Verbs

Helping verbs are verbs that help out action verbs. *Has, have, am, is, are, was, were, can,* and *will* are examples of helping verbs.

Directions: Circle the helping verb in each sentence. Write the helping verb and its action verb on the line.

1. We will go to football practice after school. _____

2. We were walking to school when it started to rain. _____

3. He can help us with the work. _____

4. Caleb is going to the dance with Lisa. _____

5. I do not like the taste of green vegetables. _____

6. Mason would go on the trip, but he is sick. _____

7. I am writing my essay for English class. _____

8. Mom is baking cookies for the girls in the club. _____

9. Marcus has seen much of Hawaii. _____

10. Frances has taken karate lesson for four years. _____

11. Molly can make puppets out of socks. _____

12. I have taken my medicine, but I am not feeling better yet. _____

13. Paul will call his grandmother tonight. _____

14. We were running in the marathon last summer. _____

15. Zoe can go with you to the mall. _____

16. Ronald has given the teacher his assignment. _____

17. Kate is taking a nap. _____

18. Will you answer my question? _____

The Same and the Opposite

Antonyms are words that have opposite or nearly opposite meanings: *huge* and *tiny*.

Synonyms are words that have the same or nearly the same meanings: *friendly* and *kind*.

Part 1

Directions: Circle the antonym for each word.

1.	skillful		
	a. adept	**b.** practiced	**c.** incompetent
2.	bright		
	a. clever	**b.** dull	**c.** shiny
3.	ancient		
	a. new	**b.** used	**c.** old
4.	imaginary		
	a. make-believe	**b.** real	**c.** fiction
5.	harsh		
	a. cruel	**b.** hard	**c.** gentle

Part 2

Directions: Circle the synonym for each word.

1.	expensive		
	a. costly	**b.** cheap	**c.** inexpensive
2.	pessimistic		
	a. optimistic	**b.** negative	**c.** positive
3.	careful		
	a. cautious	**b.** careless	**c.** uncaring
4.	colorful		
	a. dull	**b.** bleak	**c.** bright
5.	sorrowful		
	a. mournful	**b.** happy	**c.** cheerful

Commas with Appositives

Appositives are phrases in a sentence that give more information about a subject. An appositive makes the reader "positive" about who or what the writer is referring to.

Appositives include extra information; therefore, they should be set off with a comma(s) from the rest of the sentence. Since appositives give extra information about a topic, they should never come at the beginning of a sentence.

Examples

Sally, my cousin, will also be at the camp.
(*My cousin* is an appositive telling who Sally is.)

She gave a book to Rafael, the new boy in her class.
(*The new boy in her class* is an appositive telling who Rafael is.)

Directions: Add commas as needed to each sentence. Circle the appositive in each sentence.

1. You should take her class ancient history when you go to the middle school.

2. Do you think Mrs. Adams the lady with the blue dress is going to be our substitute teacher?

3. I wish you would sing that song the one with the duet part for the talent show.

4. My dog the German shepherd won first place in the dog show.

5. Have you been to Tennessee the Volunteer State to visit the Country Music Hall of Fame?

6. I want to invite Lisa my sister's best friend to my birthday party.

7. Drive south on Elm Street and turn at the library the building with the blue shutters.

8. Go sit by Donna the girl with the red hair and the glasses.

Something Extra: Write your own appositive on the lines below. Be sure to use commas correctly.

_____

_____

Writing a Business Letter

A business letter has six parts. The parts include the following: *heading*, *inside address*, *salutation*, *body*, *closing*, and *signature*.

Directions: The business letter below has a least 10 capitalization, comma, or spelling mistakes. Circle the mistakes on the page. Then on your own sheet of paper, rewrite the letter without any mistakes.

1234 Elm Lane
Sandy City MS 98765
Janruary 15 2011

Caramel Industries
89 Candy Lane
Rocky Town GA 56789

Dear Sir or madam

For the holidaze, I was given a box of your premium caramal candy. I must say, it was the best candy I have ever eaten. So often people take the time to complain, but people don't often take the time to let people know when they are doing something right. Your candy is absolutely delicious, and I just wanted to let you know I will definately be buying it and giving the candy next year for gifts to people who are on my "get-them-something-special" list.

Thank you for making such a wonderful product

Sincerely

Jackson Durmont

Writing Poetry with a Set Rhyme Scheme

A *limerick* is a humorous poem that tells a funny story about a central character. The limerick has a set rhyme scheme.

The limerick's rhyme scheme is AABBA. This means lines 1, 2, and 5 must rhyme. Lines 3 and 4 must rhyme.

Lines 1, 2, and 5 have the same rhythm. These lines have the same number or nearly the same number of syllables. These lines generally have eight, nine, or ten syllables.

Lines 3 and 4 have the same rhythm. These lines generally have five syllables.

The total length of a limerick is five lines. The last line must have a surprise or funny ending.

Limerick

There once was a beautiful dame, (A)

Who had a fierce lion to tame. (A)

She taught it to play (B)

It forgot one day (B)

That eating her wasn't the game! (A)

Directions: Use the outline below to help get started on writing a limerick.

Line 1: There once was a _____ from _____ ,

Line 2: Who _____ .

Line 3: _____

Line 4: _____

Line 5: _____ !

Something Extra: Draw a picture on a separate sheet of paper to illustrate your limerick.

Which Is Less? Which Is More?

Directions: Compare each set of fractions. Decide if the fractions are *equal to*, *less than*, or *greater than* each other. Use the pictures to help you choose the correct answer.

Write the correct symbol (**=**, **>**, or **<**) on the line.

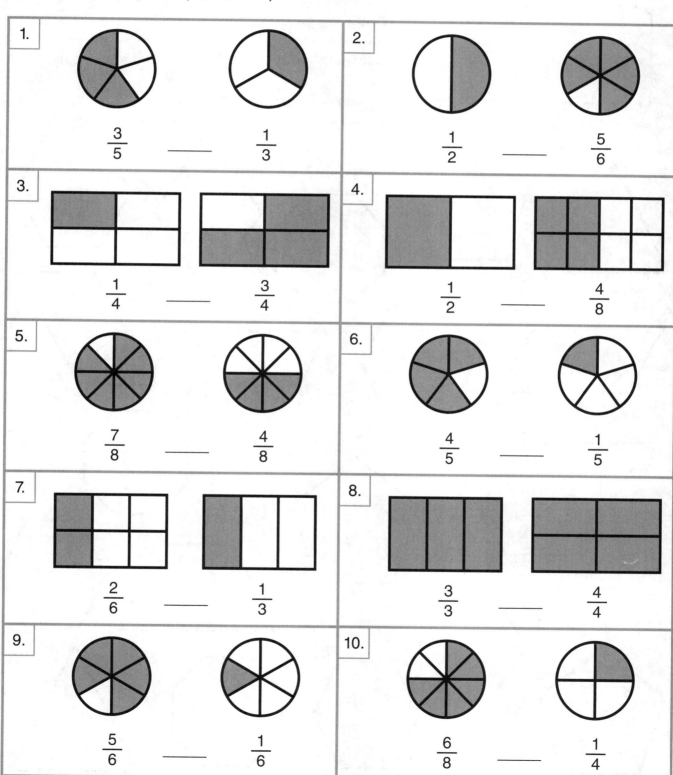

Recognizing Different Shapes

You will need crayons for this activity.

Directions: Use the Color Code to color each polygon shape on this page.

Color Code			
triangle—red	pentagon—yellow	trapezoid—blue	octagon—pink
parallelogram—violet	rhombus—green	hexagon—orange	

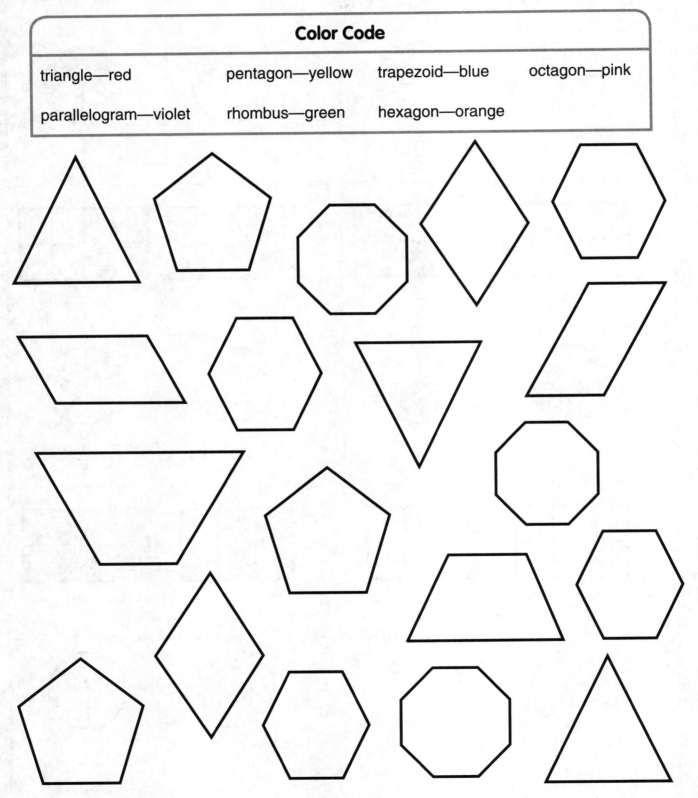

What's in a Triangle?

Directions: Find the degree of each angle that is not marked.

Hint: Remember that the sum of the interior angles of any triangle is 180°.

1.

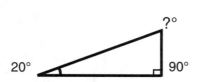

? angle = _____ degrees

2.

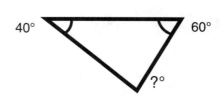

? angle = _____ degrees

3.

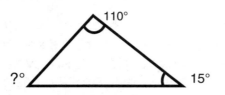

? angle = _____ degrees

4.

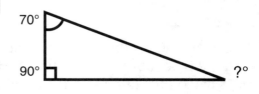

? angle = _____ degrees

5.

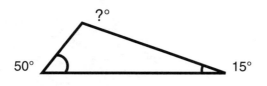

? angle = _____ degrees

6.

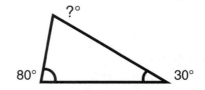

? angle = _____ degrees

7.

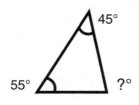

? angle = _____ degrees

8.

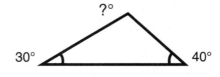

? angle = _____ degrees

#2574 *Fourth Grade Success*

What's the Deal?

Directions: Read and solve each word problem.

---

1. Mario is at the store. He wants to buy some bread. One loaf costs $2.89. Another loaf costs $3.49, but this loaf is 30% off. Which loaf of bread is the better deal?

Show your work:

Best price: _____

---

2. Irina wants to rent a hotel room for her family's vacation. She has called several hotels to get the best price. The price at Hotel A is $234 per night. Hotel A will give Karen a 20% discount if she rents the hotel room by the end of the week. Hotel B costs $189 a night, but Hotel B does not have a discount. Which hotel is the better bargain?

Show your work:

Best price: _____

---

3. Mac is planning to buy a new television. The electronics store where Mac is shopping has two televisions that appear to be good deals. One television is $789. The second television is $889. The salesperson offers Mac a 25% discount off the second television. Which television is the better buy?

Show your work:

Best price: _____

Plotting on a Graph

A *coordinate* is a point on a graph plotted using the **X**-axis and **Y**-axis. The **X**-axis is the first number of the set of paired numbers. The **Y**-axis is the second number of the set of paired numbers. When plotting on a graph, go across and then up.

Directions: Graph each coordinate in the box below. Write the corresponding letter on the graph where the point is located. The first one has been done for you.

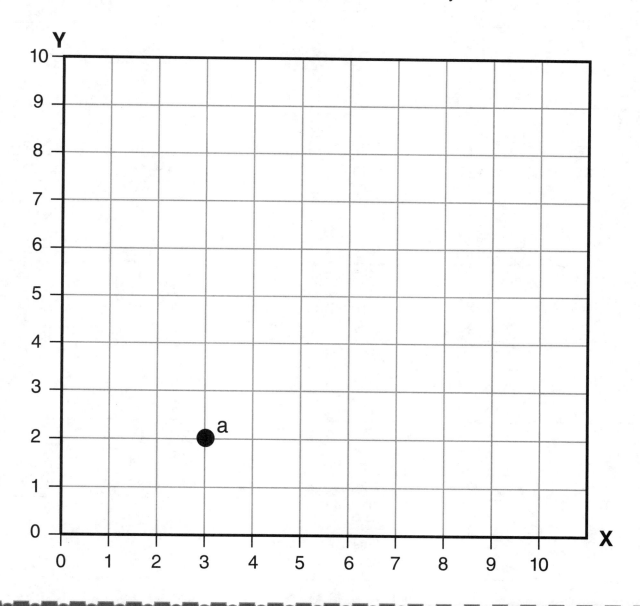

a. (3, 2)	**e.** (4, 6)	**i.** (9, 3)
b. (9, 7)	**f.** (7, 3)	**j.** (4, 2)
c. (0, 5)	**g.** (7, 2)	**k.** (0, 7)
d. (1, 6)	**h.** (6, 10)	**l.** (4,0)

Either Way, It's the Same

Directions: Check each multiplication problem by solving each set with reversed factors. Show your work.

1. 17 13 x 13 x 17	**2.** 90 21 x 21 x 90	**3.** 22 34 x 34 x 22
4. 12 81 x 81 x 12	**5.** 77 43 x 43 x 77	**6.** 10 19 x 19 x 10
7. 39 62 x 62 x 39	**8.** 13 87 x 87 x 13	**9.** 48 72 x 72 x 48
10. 22 58 x 58 x 22	**11.** 88 29 x 29 x 88	**12.** 44 39 x 39 x 44
13. 17 50 x 50 x 17	**14.** 77 33 x 33 x 77	**15.** 35 67 x 67 x 35

Turning Fractions into Decimals

You can divide a fraction's numerator by its denominator to create an equivalent decimal.

Example

$$\frac{4}{5} \rightarrow 5\overline{)4.0}^{\,0.8}$$

Directions: Use the space provided to work each problem. Add the decimal point as needed. Round to the nearest hundredth.

1. $\frac{8}{9}$	2. $\frac{9}{18}$	3. $\frac{6}{7}$
4. $\frac{12}{20}$	5. $\frac{5}{8}$	6. $\frac{3}{10}$
7. $\frac{2}{9}$	8. $\frac{4}{7}$	9. $\frac{1}{8}$
10. $\frac{2}{3}$	11. $\frac{3}{5}$	12. $\frac{5}{6}$
13. $\frac{1}{3}$	14. $\frac{7}{9}$	15. $\frac{4}{8}$

Answer Key for Bonus Section

Page 178
1. "I wish," Tom said, "I could go with you."
2. "Do you think," Melinda asked, "this is the right one?"
3. "Maybe tomorrow," Jada said, "we'll finally learn the answer."
4. "I believe," Mrs. Sanders said, "you need to be more careful when writing your answers."
5. "Have you ever," asked Margaret, "been to Europe?"
6. "Maybe," Mom said, "you can invite some of your friends over next Friday."
7. "Something special," said Mia's father, "is going to happen on your birthday."
8. "Why," asked Kate, "does it always seem to rain on the weekends?"
9. "If you ever get to Boston," Tina said, "be sure to visit me."
10. "You," Andrea said, "are my best friend."

Something Extra: Answers will vary.

Page 179
1. Whose   2. compliment   3. cite   4. immigrants
5. a lot   6. all ready   7. breath   8. led
9. lose   10. passed

Page 180
1. will go   2. were walking   3. can help
4. is going   5. do (not) like   6. would go
7. am writing   8. is baking   9. has seen
10. has taken   11. can make   12. have taken, am (not) feeling
13. will call   14. were running
15. can go   16. has given   17. is taking
18. will (you) answer

Page 181
Part 1
1. c   2. b   3. a   4. b   5. c
Part 2
1. a   2. b   3. a   4. c   5. a

Page 182
1. You should take her class, ancient history, when you go to the middle school.
2. Do you think Mrs. Adams, the lady with the blue dress, is going to be our substitute teacher?
3. I wish you would sing that song, the one with the duet part, for the talent show.
4. My dog, the German shepherd, won first place in the dog show.
5. Have you been to Tennessee, the Volunteer State, to visit the Country Music Hall of Fame?
6. I want to invite Lisa, my sister's best friend, to my birthday party.
7. Drive south on Elm Street and turn at the library, the building with the blue shutters.
8. Go sit by Donna, the girl with the red hair and the glasses.

Something Extra: Answers will vary.

Page 183 Suggested corrections
Sandy City, MS 98765
January 15, 2011
Rocky Town, GA 56789
Dear Sir or Madam:
For the holidays, I was given a box of your premium caramel candy.
Your candy is absolutely delicious, and I just wanted to let you know. I will definitely be buying it and giving the candy next year for gifts to people who are on my "get-them- something-special" list.
Thank you for making such a wonderful product.
Sincerely,

Page 184
Answers will vary. Rhyme scheme must be AABBA.
Something Extra: Answers will vary.

Page 185
1. >   2. <   3. <   4. =   5. >
6. >   7. =   8. =   9. >   10. >

Page 186

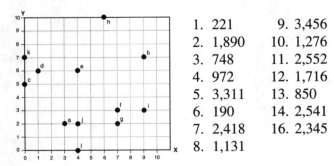

Page 187
1. 70°
2. 80°
3. 55°
4. 20°
5. 115°
6. 70°
7. 80°
8. 110°

Page 188
1. The loaf that is 30% off is the better deal because it costs $2.44.
2. Hotel A is the better bargain. The cost with the discount is $187.20.
3. The second television, with the 25% discount, is the better buy; the final cost is $666.75.

Page 189

Page 190
1. 221   9. 3,456
2. 1,890   10. 1,276
3. 748   11. 2,552
4. 972   12. 1,716
5. 3,311   13. 850
6. 190   14. 2,541
7. 2,418   16. 2,345
8. 1,131

Page 191
1. .89   2. .5   3. .86   4. .6   5. .63
6. .3   7. .22   8. .57   9. .13   10. .67
11. .6   12. .83   13. .33   14. .78   15. .5